Head to Toe
Crochet

HERBERT PRESS
Bloomsbury Publishing Plc
50 Bedford Square, London, WC1B 3DP, UK
29 Earlsfort Terrace, Dublin 2, Ireland

BLOOMSBURY, HERBERT PRESS and the Herbert Press logo
are trademarks of Bloomsbury Publishing Plc

First published in Great Britain in 2022

A catalogue record for this book is available from the British Library

ISBN 978-1-78994-045-9; eBook: 978-1-78994-046-6

2 4 6 8 10 9 7 5 3 1

Produced and designed for Bloomsbury by Plum5 Limited
Edited by Rachel Vowles and Helen Welch

Model photography © Tiny Toes by Aggi Photography Studio
Step-by-step photographs by Roxanne Bennett, Scarlett McQueen and Charlie West
All other incidental images © Shutterstock

Printed and bound in China by Toppan Leefung Printing

To find out more about our authors and books visit www.bloomsbury.com
and sign up for our newsletters

Head to Toe
Crochet

Beanies and Booties for Infants to Toddlers

GURINDER KAUR HATCHARD

HERBERT PRESS

LONDON • OXFORD • NEW YORK • NEW DELHI • SYDNEY

To my amazingly
creative and talented
mum, Amarjit.

Thank you for everything.
Love you always x

CONTENTS

INTRODUCTION

The arrival of a baby can inspire such wonderful crafting from all those around them. Whether you have never crocheted before and want to create something special and handmade for the new baby in your life or you're a seasoned crocheter and want some new ideas for fun patterns, this is the book for you.

Within these pages, you'll find a range of super cute matching beanie hats and booties, so that you can create a fabulous gift set for the new baby in your life. Little monsters, tigers and dogs are just some of the creations you can get your hooks into, which fit right from the very start of babyhood to the first year, and possibly beyond. The beanies and booties stand out so expect lots of lovely "oohs" and "aahs" when the adorable little one is out and about.

As they are quite small, once you've got the hang of crocheting, these projects can be whipped up fairly quickly, which comes in handy if you are time poor.

Remember, the colours I've included in this book are only a suggestion. Why not break with convention and get experimental with your makes – who says your fox can't be purple or your ladybird can't be blue? Children love weird and wonderful creations!

My mum taught me to crochet when I was eight years old and, although it took a while to get the stitches right, I was always amazed at how a simple ball of yarn could be transformed into the most intricate design. My skills lay dormant for a few years but when I was pregnant with my first child I wanted to create something unique for her and was inspired to crochet again. By the time baby number two came along, I was fully immersed in crochet and started designing so I could go beyond the traditional patterns. The creations that you find in these pages are inspired by this joy of seeing babies in modern and bright crocheted items.

I hope you enjoy making these crocheted creations!
Happy Crocheting!

Gurinder
x

GETTING STARTED

YARNS

If you're a first time crocheter you may find the sheer amount of choice when it comes to yarn overwhelming and not be sure of which yarn is best for your project.

For ease, all the patterns in the book use the same weight of yarn, DK Yarn, which is also knowns as double knitting or Light Worsted Weight yarn. This means that you can get a few basic colours in this weight and use them across the different patterns. It's an easy to handle weight of yarn and is not too fine or chunky if you're new to crochet.

Yarns are available to buy in an eye-watering range of fibres, well beyond sheep's wool. Before you buy, remember to check for the washing instructions, and if you're giving these as a gift you may wish to jot them down for the parents so they can refer to them later. Whichever fibre you choose, check that they are all the same weight.

Acrylic yarn is a man-made fibre and is usually cheaper than natural alternatives.

It's hardwearing and washing machine friendly. You can get special furry or fluffy yarns which may suit some of your creations.

Wool is lovely to use, with Merino known for being the softest. Be aware that a very small number of babies can be born with lanolin allergies. As well as sheep, alpacas are also great providers of yarn and their yarn is hypoallergenic and has thermal properties.

Bamboo is plant-based and a renewable resource. It's also know for its antibacterial quality and is hypoallergenic. It's often blended with other fibres like cotton to create robust accessories for babies. If you're crocheting something as a gift for vegan parents a cotton and bamboo blend would be a good choice.

HOOKS
Crochet hooks can be found in a few different materials including bamboo, plastic and aluminium. Good standard metal crochet hooks tend to be the easiest to get started with.

You'll generally find the size of the hook printed onto it in the middle.

The patterns in this book are usually quite quick to finish, but if you're going to be doing a lot of crochet or are prone to repetitive strain injuries, a hook with an ergonomic handle may be best for you.

Most of the patterns in this book are created with either a 4mm (G-6) or 3.5mm (E-4) size hook. Using the smaller hook (3.5mm) for the booties will create a slightly tighter and sturdier shoe which holds its shape better. Check the tension when you begin as you may need to use a slightly different size hook.

OTHER SUPPLIES

TAPESTRY/YARN NEEDLES

These are blunt with a large eye for threading yarn through. You'll need these for sewing on all the embellishments of your pieces, a little bit of basic embroidery and for weaving in those dreaded loose ends!

SCISSORS

Keep a pair handy with you for snipping your yarn – using your teeth as a substitute is not recommended!

STITCH MARKERS

There are only a few patterns in this book that will require one. If you don't have one handy,

just use a small piece of yarn in a contrasting colour.

TAPE MEASURE

This will help you keep track of your measurements as you go along.

STUFFING

A few of the patterns require some stuffing. A zero-waste option would be to consider just saving all your little scraps of yarn that you've snipped off and using them or using (clean!) old tights or bits of ripped up t-shirts. If you're planning on creating a lot of other projects that require stuffing you may want to consider buying a large bag of polyester stuffing.

SCALES

Because I am a yarn-buying addict and I'm trying to overcome this and stop others from falling into the same trap, I have indicated as much as possible the smallest amount of yarn you'll need for a pattern. There's no need to buy 100g when you'll only use 10g, so if you have scrap balls of yarn from other projects weigh them before you go out and buy more. Or just keep buying more yarn because it's beautiful and squishy!

SIZING

Babies come in all shapes and sizes and grow at different rates so please use the sizing as a guide only.

HATS	Size A (preemie)	Size B (baby 0-3 months)	Size B* (3-6 months) see notes below	Size C (6 months – Toddler)
Circumference (cm)	29.5	36	40	42
Length (inches)	11½	14	15¾	16½
Length (cm)	10	12	14.5	16
Length (inches)	4	4¾	5¾	6½

*If you require a size 3-6 months, use the instructions for size B with a 5mm hook (tension: 13 sts x 7 rows = 10cm/4in measured over treble crochet).

BOOTIES (length of sole)	Size A (0-6 months)	Size B (6-9 months)	Size C (9-12 months)
cm	9.5	11.5	12.5
inches	3¾	4½	5

HOW TO CROCHET

If you've never crocheted before, or you're brushing up on skills that have lain dormant for years, please be patient with yourself – crochet wasn't built in a day! Get comfortable with some of the basic techniques first before you start a project. I've provided a guide here, but you may also find video tutorials helpful too. You'll find some on my website, www.yayforcrochet.com.

HOLDING YOUR HOOK

There are two ways to hold a hook, the pencil position and the knife position. If you're new to crochet it's worth trying both positions out and seeing which is more comfortable. The hook is held in your dominant hand.

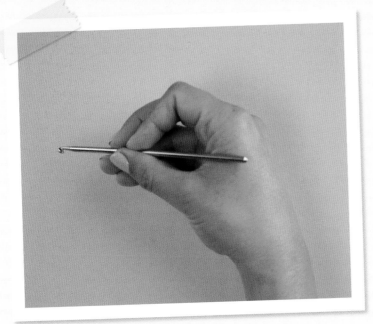

PENCIL POSITION
Hold the hook as you would if it was a pencil, around 3-5cm/1¼-2in from the tip, or if your hook has a thumb rest, hold it here.

KNIFE POSITION
Hold the hook as if you were cutting up food with a table knife, around 3-5cm/1¼-2in from the tip, or if your hook has a thumb rest, hold it here.

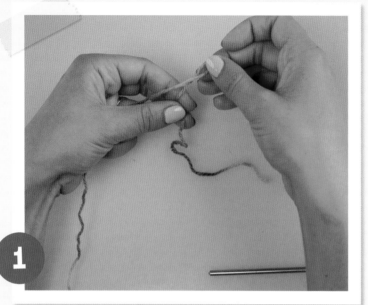

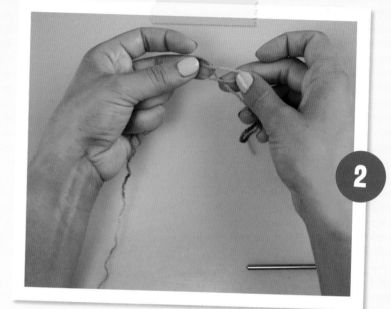

Unless otherwise stated, all the projects in this book begin with a slip knot. Make a loop with the yarn.

Take the piece that is on top and fold it underneath the loop.

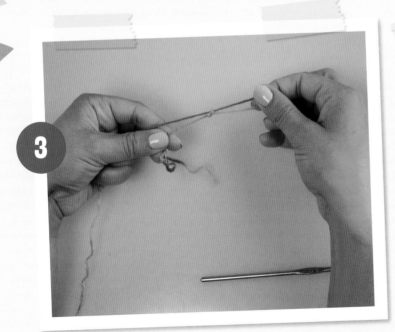

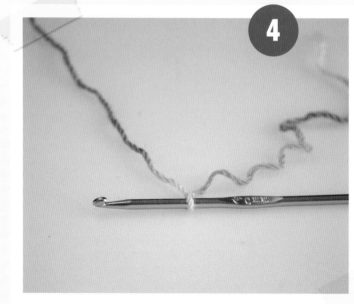

Pull this piece through the loop to create the slip knot.

Put the crochet hook into the loop and pull the yarn end so that the loop is close to the hook but not too tight. Check that you can still move the hook easily.

HOLDING YOUR YARN

The yarn is held with your non-dominant hand. My preferred method for holding yarn is to hold your hand as if you are about to click your fingers. There are other methods so see which is the most comfortable for you.

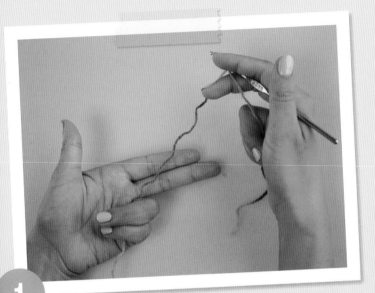

1 At around 20cm/8in from the yarn end, hold the yarn to your palm with your little finger and ring finger, securely but not too tight so you can't pull up the yarn.

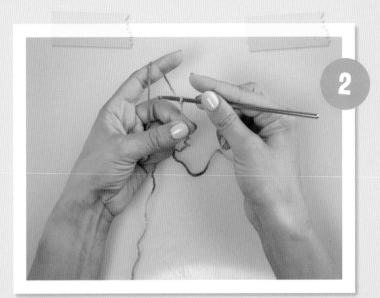

2 Hang the yarn on your index finger and bring your thumb and middle finger in to pinch the yarn just under the slip knot.

3 As your work progresses your index finger and thumb should move along sitting just under the loop your crochet hook is in.

CHAIN STITCH
(abbreviation: ch)

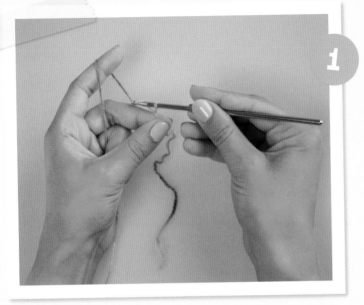

After you've started with a slip knot, hold the hook in your dominant hand, wrap the yarn around the hook so it is gripped by the tip.

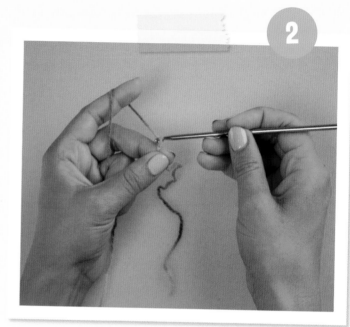

Pull this yarn through your slip knot.

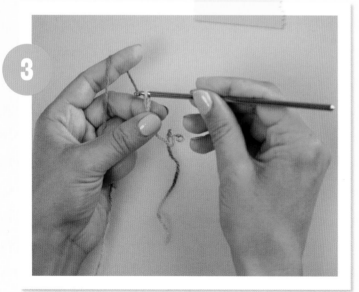

Continue to create more stitches with this method, wrapping the yarn around the hook and pulling it through the loop that is already on your hook. They will look like a small plait.

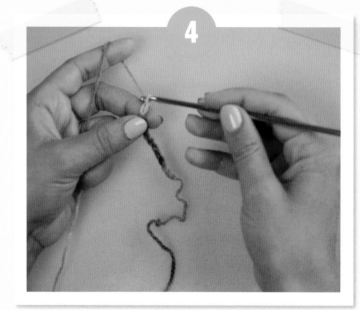

Move the thumb and middle finger of your non-dominant hand up to just under the loop as you continue working.

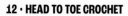

SLIP STITCH

(abbreviation: sl st)

Slip stitches are used to join rounds or to move to another point on your work.

Insert the hook into the stitch.

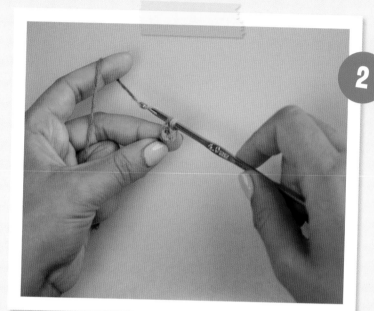

Wrap the yarn around the tip of the hook.

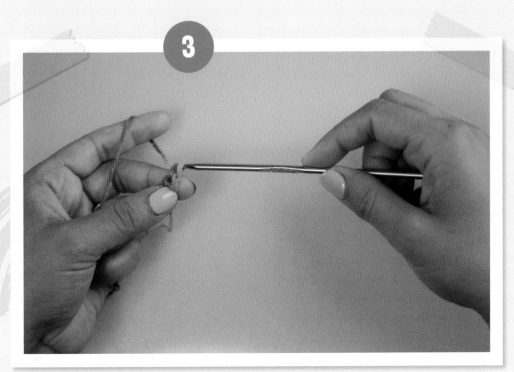

Pull the yarn through the stitch and through the loop on the hook.

DOUBLE CROCHET (single crochet in US)

(abbreviation: dc)

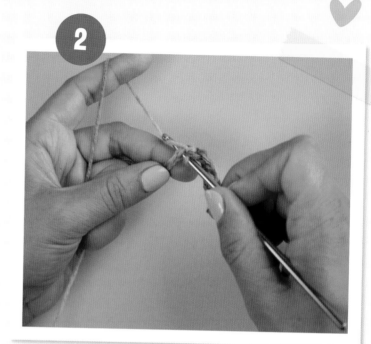

Insert the hook into the stitch.

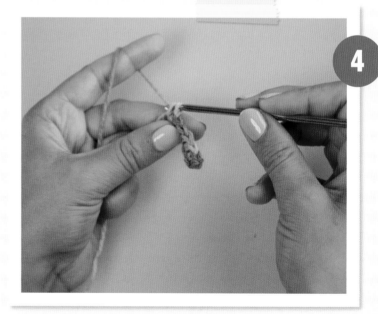

Wrap the yarn around the hook.

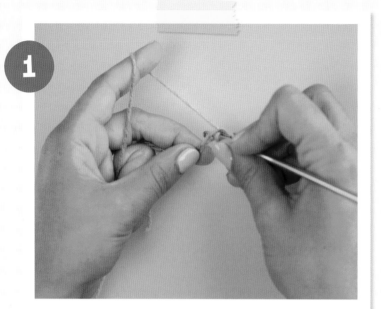

Pull this through the stitch. There will now be two loops on the hook.

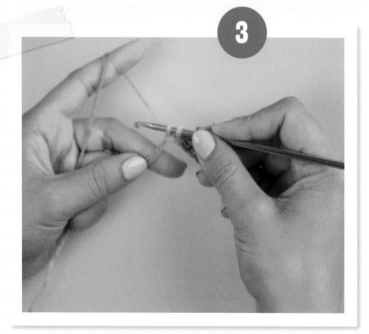

Wrap the yarn over the hook again and pull it through both loops.

HALF TREBLE CROCHET (half double crochet in US)

(abbreviation: htr)

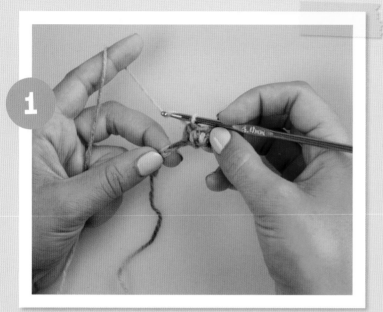

Wrap the yarn around the hook.

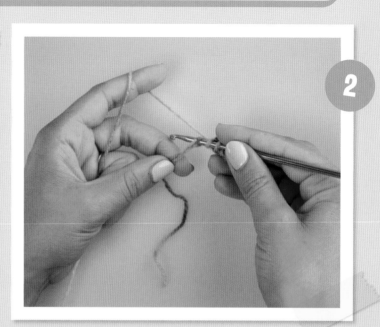

Insert the hook into the stitch.

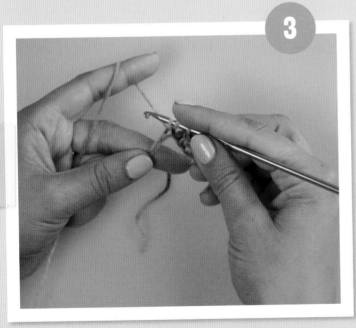

Wrap the yarn around the hook and pull it through the stitch. You will now have three loops on the hook.

Wrap the yarn around the hook and pull it through all three loops.

In your pattern, the 2 chain at the start of a row or round counts as one half treble.

TREBLE CROCHET (double crochet in US)

(abbreviation: tr)

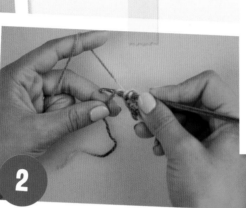

1 Wrap the yarn around the hook.

2 Insert the hook into the stitch.

3 Wrap the yarn around the hook and pull it through the stitch. You will now have three loops on the hook.

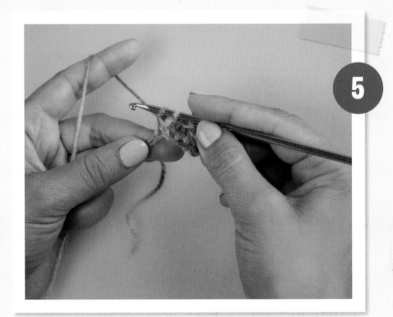

4 Wrap the yarn around the hook and pull it through the first two loops.

5 You will now have two loops on your hook. Wrap the yarn around the hook and pull this through both loops.

6 In your pattern, the 3 chain at the start of a row or round count as a treble.

DOUBLE TREBLE CROCHET (treble crochet in the US)

(abbreviation: dtr)

1 Wrap the yarn twice around the hook.

2 Insert the hook into the stitch.

3 Wrap the yarn around the hook and pull it through the stitch. You will now have four loops on the hook.

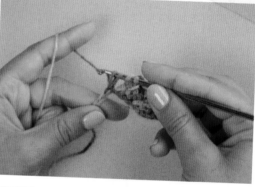

Wrap the yarn around the hook and pull it through the first two loops.

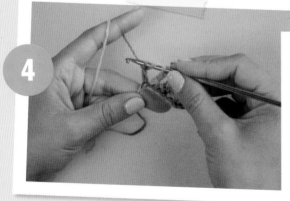

4 You will now have three loops on your hook. Wrap the yarn around the hook and pull it through the first two loops.

5

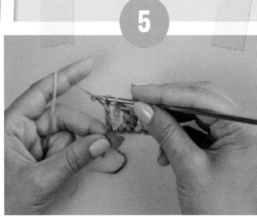

You will now have two loops on your hook. Wrap the yarn around the hook and pull it through both remaining loops.

HALF TREBLE CROCHET DECREASE
(half double crochet decrease in US)

(abbreviation: htr2tog)

1 Wrap the yarn around the hook, and insert the hook into the stitch.

2 Pull the yarn through. You will now have three loops on your hook.

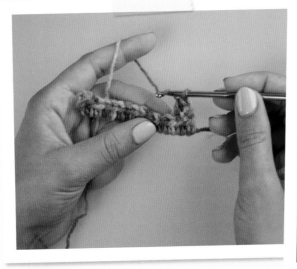

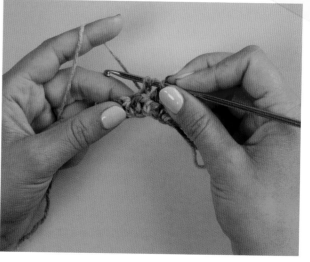

3 Wrap the yarn around the hook and insert the hook into the next stitch.

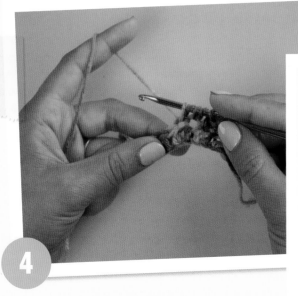

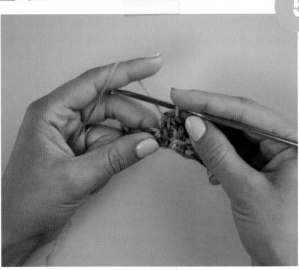

5 Wrap the yarn around the hook and pull this through all five loops.

6 When you are counting your stitches at the end of a row or round, this counts as one stitch.

4 Pull the yarn through. You will now have five loops on your stitch.

TREBLE CROCHET DECREASE
(double crochet decrease in US)
(abbreviation: tr2tog)

1 Wrap the yarn around the hook and insert the hook into the stitch.

2 Pull the yarn through. You will now have three loops on your hook.

3 Wrap the yarn around the hook and pull through the first two loops. You will now have two loops on your hook.

4 Wrap the yarn around the hook and insert into the next stitch. Pull the yarn through. You will now have four loops on your hook.

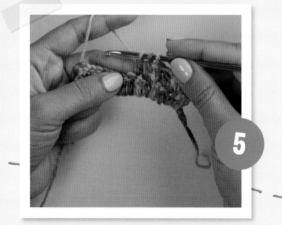

5 Wrap the yarn around the hook and pull through the first two loops. You will now have three loops on your hook.

6 Wrap the yarn around the hook and pull it through all three loops.

7 When you are counting your stitches at the end of a row or round, this counts as one stitch.

BACK LOOPS ONLY

(abbreviation: blo)

All the booties call for a round to be completed in back loops only. When you are normally crocheting you put your hook through the two loops of a stitch.

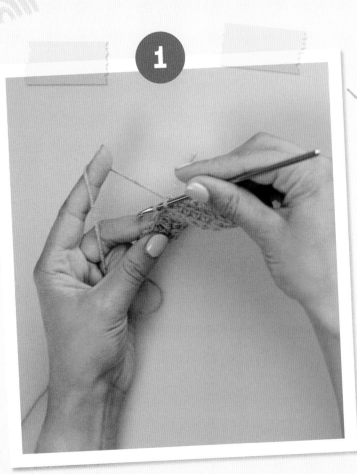

When you need to do back loops only, find the one loop at the back of the stitch and put your hook through this one only.

Finish the stitch.

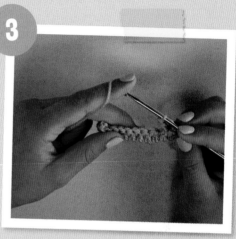

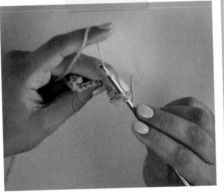

2 Wrap the yarn around the hook and pull this through behind the treble.

3 You will now have three loops on your hook. Continue to crochet a treble as normal.

1 Wrap the yarn around the hook and instead of inserting into the stitch, insert the hook from the front, then behind the treble of the previous row/round, and back out to the front again on the other side of the stitch.

WORKING IN THE ROUND

Most of the patterns in this book are worked in the round. Always be sure to complete each round with a slip stitch and join this to the top of the starting chain.

WORKING IN ROWS

If you're working in rows, remember to turn at the end of a row. You do not have to join with a slip stitch.

TENSION

It's always recommended to create a tension square before you start any wearable projects as everyone will make their stitches at slightly different sizes. Crochet a square swatch that is slightly larger than 10 x 10cm/4 x4in. Measure 10cm/4in and see if you have the same number of stitches that is stated at the start of the pattern. If you have more stitches than specified in the pattern, your tension is too tight and you'll need to increase the size of your hook. If you have fewer stitches than the pattern states, you'll need to use a slightly smaller hook. Create another tension swatch to test again.

MAGIC RING

Also known as an adjustable loop. When a very tight start is necessary, a magic ring is used as an alternative to the slip knot.

At around 10cm/4in from the yarn end, wrap the yarn twice around your index and middle fingers.

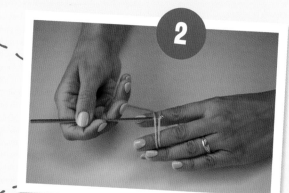

Insert the hook under both loops, pull the yarn closest to your knuckles under the other one.

Use your dominant hand to take the yarn off your fingers, while keeping the shape.

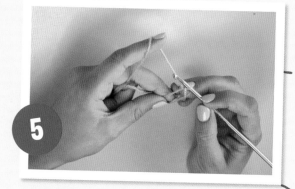

Hold the loose ring with the thumb and middle finger of your non-dominant hand, wrap the yarn around the hook and pull through (as if you are creating a chain).

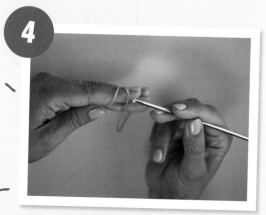

When you've finished the pattern instructions, pull the yarn end and the ring will tighten.

Follow the instructions in your pattern and crochet all the stitches into the loose ring. Join with a slip stitch if required in the pattern.

BLOCKING

Blocking isn't necessary for most of the hats and booties in this book. The exception to this is the soccer hat. The pieces will retain their shape a lot better with blocking. Pin the hexagons and pentagons onto a padded board like an ironing board. Spray lightly with water and leave to dry under a towel.

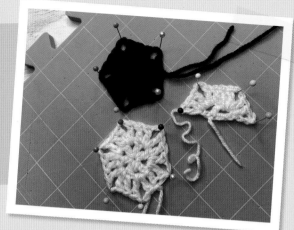

CONVERSION TABLE (ABBREVIATIONS)

This book is written using UK terminology. If you're looking at tutorials on the internet, check which countries' terms they are using so you don't end up with the wrong stitches in your work.

UK TERM	US TERM
Chain (ch)	Chain (ch)
Slip stitch (sl st)	Slip stitch (sl st or ss)
Double crochet (dc)	Single crochet (sc)
Half treble crochet (htr)	Half double crochet (hdc)
Treble crochet (tr)	Double crochet (dc)
Double treble crochet (dtr)	Treble crochet (tr)

HOW TO READ A PATTERN

To the untrained eye, crochet patterns can look quite daunting. Once you know how to decode them, they are fairly easy to read.

Unless the pattern says to use a magic ring, always start with a slip knot.

Start your pattern with 5 chain stitches and join with a slip stitch to form a ring.

The numbers in brackets within the pattern indicate the different sizes. In the example shown, for preemie you would crochet 9 trebles, and for newborn and 6-12 months you would crochet 11 trebles.

The "ch" at the start of a row or round gives you the height you'll need. 3 chain count as a treble, 2 chain count as a half treble.

A number and a stitch (eg 4tr) means that you crochet 1 treble in each of the next 4 stitches.

EXAMPLE

5ch. Join with a sl st in first ch to form a ring.

Rnd 1: 3ch (counts as first tr here and throughout), 9 (11, 11)tr in ring, join - 10 (12, 12) sts.

Rnd 2: 3ch, [2tr in next st] 9 [11, 11] times, 1tr in same st as starting 3 ch, join - 20 (24, 24) sts.

Rnd 3: 3ch, [2tr in next st, 1tr] 9 [11, 11] times, 2tr in next st, join - 30 (36, 36) sts.

Rnd 4: 3ch, 4tr, 1htr to end - 30 (36, 36) sts.

Rnd 5: 3ch, 4tr, *2tr in next st, 1ch, 3tr, rpt from * to end – 40 (48, 48) sts.

This means repeat the stitches from where the asterix * appears until the end of your round.

The numbers at the end of the row or round, after the dash, indicate what your stitch count should be when you have finished that row or round. The first number is for the smallest size, second is for the middle size and so on.

Square brackets indicate that this section should be repeated however many times stated.

"Join" at the end of a line means join with a slip stitch to the top of the starting chain. If you started with 3 ch, work the slip stitch into the top (or 3rd) of these 3 ch.

"Htr to end" means that you carry on this stitch until the end of the row or round. This may also be written as "1htr in each st around".

CHARTS

These charts provide a visual representation of how to get started on the basic beanie hat and the sole of the bootie. Both are shown in newborn size.

KEY

• slip stitch

⬭ chain

⊤ treble

∨ 2 trebles in same st

BEANIE

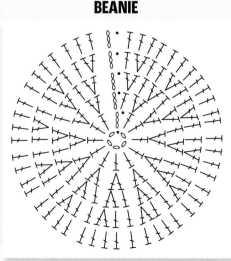

BOOTIE

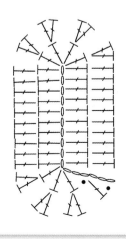

OTHER THINGS TO NOTE

- Instructions for the booties are just written for one shoe (although the yarn amounts given are enough for a pair) so when you've finished one shoe, repeat the process for the other shoe.

- These shoes are not intended to be worn for walking, and are not slip resistant.

- When creating all the little appliqués like eyes and noses, leave enough yarn for sewing.

SUPPLIERS

It's too hard for me to pick a favourite yarn brand but I can heartily recommend Paintbox Yarns, Stylecraft Yarns, Red Heart, Knitcraft, James C Brett, and Sirdar.
There are plenty more too, as well as thousands of amazing indie dyers across the world.

YARN SHOPS

I would highly recommend buying your supplies from a bricks and mortar store because it's great to actually squish potential yarn and get a good feel for it before you buy it. Local yarn stores are run by dedicated and experienced crafters who can offer their expertise to help you.
UK Hand Knitting Association directory: www.ukhandknitting.com
America's Knitting Yarn Shop directory: www.americasknitting.com

ARTS AND CRAFT CHAIN STORES

Hobbycraft is the UK's largest craft chain. They supply yarn from well-known brands as well as their exclusive Women's Institute yarn and their own brand Knitcraft, both of which have a huge range of colours in DK weight so would be suitable for all the patterns in this book. www.hobbycraft.co.uk
Online suppliers (UK)
Love Crafts
www.lovecrafts.com
Wool Warehouse
www.woolwarehouse.co.uk

ETSY

A great place to find small, independent yarn brands (and millions of other things!)
www.etsy.com

FRIENDS AND FAMILY

You may find that someone in your life has lots of unused yarn in their stash. As some of the projects only require tiny amounts of certain colours, ask if they can bear to part with some, so you can put it to good use. Charity shops are also good places to have a look for yarn.

FOREST FOX BEANIE

As foxes and babies are both very nocturnal creatures this seems like a good fit. The rust-coloured yarn could be a great choice for Autumn born babies.

YARN

Size A (B, C)

● 25g (25g, 50g) DK Rust

○ 25g DK White

Scrap yarn DK Black

SIZES

A: Preemie
B: Newborn – 3 months
C: 6 months – 1 year and beyond

TOOLS

4mm hook
Tapestry needle

TENSION

10 sts x 8 rows = 10cm/4in
measured over treble crochet

PATTERN NOTES

- Apart from the snout, everything in this pattern is crocheted in the round. At the end of every round slip stitch to the top chain from start of the row.

- When you've fastened off the nose, ears, eyes and snout leave enough yarn for sewing.

BEANIE

With rust

5ch. Join with a sl st in first ch to form a ring.

Rnd 1: 3ch (counts as first tr here and throughout), 9 (11, 11)tr in ring, join - 10 (12, 12) sts.

Rnd 2: 3ch, [2tr in next st] 9 [11, 11] times, 1tr in same st as starting 3 ch, join - 20 (24, 24) sts.

Rnd 3: 3ch, [2tr in next st, 1tr] 9 [11, 11] times, 2tr in next st, join - 30 (36, 36) sts.

Rnd 4: 3ch, [2tr in next st, 2tr] 9 [11, 11] times, 2tr in next st, 1tr, join - 40 (48, 48) sts.

SIZE A ONLY

Rnd 5: 3ch, 1tr in each st around, join - 40 sts.
Fasten off.
With white
Rnds 6-8: 3ch, 1tr in each st around, join.
Fasten off.

SIZE B ONLY

Rnds 5-6: 3ch, 1tr in each st around, join - 48 sts.
Fasten off.
With white
Rnds 7-10: 3ch, 1tr in each st around, join.
Fasten off. If making for a child over 2 months, crochet an 11th round.

SIZE C ONLY

Rnd 5: 3ch, [2tr in next st, 3tr] 11 times, 2tr in next st, 2tr, join - 60 sts.
Rnds 6-9: 3ch, 1tr in each st around, join.
Fasten off.
With white
Rnds 10-14: 3ch, 1tr in each st around, join.
Fasten off.

EARS

(make 2)
With rust

SIZE A ONLY

Rnd 1: 3ch, 5htr in first ch, join - 6 sts.
Rnd 2: 2ch, 2htr in each of next 5 sts, 1htr in same st as starting 2 ch, join - 12 sts.
Rnd 3: 2ch, [2htr in next st, 1htr] 5 times, 2htr in next st, join - 18 sts.
Rnd 4: 2ch, 1htr in each st around, join.
Fasten off.

SIZE B ONLY

Rnd 1: 4ch, 5tr in first ch, join with sl st to 3rd ch - 6 sts.
Rnd 2: 3ch, 2tr in each of next 5 sts, 1tr in same st as starting ch, join - 12 sts.
Rnd 3: 3ch, [2tr in next st, 1tr] 5 times, 2tr in next st, join - 18 sts.
Rnd 4: 3ch, 1tr in each st, join.
Fasten off.

SIZE C ONLY

Rnd 1: 4ch, 5tr in first ch, join with

sl st to 3rd ch - 6 sts.
Rnd 2: 3ch, 2tr in each of next 5 sts, 1tr in same st as starting ch, join - 12 sts.
Rnd 3: 3ch, [2tr in next st, 1tr] 5 times, 2tr in next st, join - 18 sts.
Rnd 4: 3ch, [2tr in next st, 2tr] 5 times, 2tr in next st, 1tr, join - 24 sts.
Rnd 5: 3ch, 1tr in each st around, join.
Fasten off.

SNOUT

With rust
Work in rows:

SIZE A AND B ONLY

Row 1: 3ch, 2htr in first ch. Turn - 3 sts.
Row 2: 2ch, 1htr in same st as 2ch, 1htr, 2htr in last st. Turn - 5 sts.
Row 3: 2ch, 1htr in same st as 2ch, 3htr, 2htr in last st. Turn - 7 sts.
If making size A fasten off.
Row 4: 2ch, 1htr in same st as 2ch, 5htr, 2htr in last st - 9 sts.
Fasten off.

SIZE C ONLY

Row 1: 4ch, 2tr in first ch. Turn - 3 sts.
Row 2: 3ch, 1tr in same st as 3ch, 1tr, 2tr in last st. Turn - 5 sts.
Row 3: 3ch, 1tr in same st as 3ch, 3tr, 2tr in last st. Turn - 7 sts.
Row 4: 3ch, 1tr in same st as 3ch, 5tr, 2tr in last st - 9 sts.
Fasten off.

NOSE AND EYES

(make 3)
With black

SIZE A ONLY

Row 1: 3ch, 5htr in first ch, join - 6 sts.
Fasten off.

SIZE B AND C ONLY

Row 1: 4ch, 5 (7)tr in first ch, join - 6 (8) sts.
Fasten off.

Sew ears, eyes, snout and nose onto the beanie. Weave in ends.

FOREST FOX BOOTIES

YARN

● 25g DK Rust

○ 10g DK White

Scrap yarn DK Black

SIZES

A: Newborn – 3 months
B: 3 months – 6 months
C: 6 months – 1 year

TOOLS

3.5mm hook
Tapestry needle

TENSION

9 sts x 4 rows = 6cm/2¼in measured over treble crochet

PATTERN NOTES

· Instructions are for one bootie, so repeat for the second.

· Instead of using the black yarn for eyes you could use small black buttons.

· The face is not crocheted in the round, so turn at the end of each row.

· The instructions for the face are the same for all the sizes of bootie.

BOOTIES

With white

Rnd 1: 13 (15, 17)ch, 1tr in 4th ch from hook, 1tr in each of next 8 (10, 12)ch, 6tr in last ch, working back along the other side of chain work 8 (10, 12)tr, 4tr in same st as first tr of rnd, join - 28 (32, 36) sts.

Rnd 2: 3ch (counts as first tr), 10 (12, 14)tr, 2tr in each of next 4 sts, 10 (12, 14)tr, 2tr in each of next 3 sts, 1tr in same st as starting 3 ch, join - 36 (40, 44) sts.

With rust

Rnd 3: 2ch (counts as first htr), 1htr blo in each st around, join.

Rnd 4: 2ch, 7 (9, 11) htr, [htr2tog, 1htr] 6 times, 10 (12, 14) htr, join - 30 (34, 38) sts.

Rnd 5: 2ch, 7 (9, 11)htr, [htr2tog,

1htr] 4 times, 10 (12, 14)htr, join - 26 (30, 34) sts.

Rnd 6: 2ch, 5 (7, 9)htr, [htr2tog] 6 times, 8 (10, 12)htr, join - 20 (24, 28) sts.

Rnd 7: 2ch, 7 (9, 11)htr, [htr2tog] twice, 8 (10, 12)htr, join - 18 (22, 26) sts.

SIZE A AND B ONLY

Rnds 8-9: 2ch, 1htr in each st to end, join.
Fasten off.

SIZE C ONLY

Rnd 8: 2ch, 9htr, [htr2tog] 4 times, 1htr in each st to end, join - 22 sts.

Rnd 9-10: 2ch, 1htr in each st to end, join.
Fasten off.

CHEEKS

(make 2)
With white
Magic ring, 2ch, 5htr in ring. Do not join - 6 sts.
Fasten off.
Sew onto the sides of fox face.

SNOUT

With black
Magic ring, 2ch, 5dc in ring, join - 6 sts.
Fasten off.

TAIL

With white
Rnd 1: Magic ring, 3ch, 7 (9, 9)tr in ring, join - 8 (10, 10) sts.
With rust
Rnds 2-4: 2ch, 1htr in each st to end, join.
For size A only, fasten off.

FOR SIZE B AND C ONLY

Rnd 5: 2ch, 1htr in each st to end, join.
Fasten off.
Leave enough yarn for sewing.

Sew the eyes and nose onto the face. Sew the tail onto the back of the shoe. Weave in ends.

FACE

With rust
Work in rows.
Row 1: 3ch, 3htr in first ch. Turn - 4 sts.
Row 2: 2ch, 1htr in same st as 2ch, 2htr, 2htr in last st. Turn - 6 sts.
Row 3: 2ch, 1htr in same st as 2ch, 4htr, 2htr in last st. Turn - 8 sts.
Row 4: 2ch, 1htr in same st as 2ch, 6htr, 2htr in last st, Turn - 10 sts.
Rows 5-6: 2ch, 1htr in each st to end. Turn
Row 7: 5ch, (work next sts back along 5 ch to create a triangle) 1dc in 2nd ch from hook, 1htr in next ch, 2tr, miss next 3 sts of main row, sl st in each of next 3 sts of main row, 5ch, (work next sts back along these 5 ch to create second triangle) 1dc in 2nd ch from hook, 1htr, 2tr, sl st in last st of main row.
Fasten off, leave a long tail for sewing.

EYES

(make 2)
With black
Magic ring, 2ch, 3dc in ring, join - 4 sts.
Fasten off.

BASSET HOUND BEANIE

The Basset Hound was TV Detective Columbo's pet of choice, Marilyn Monroe owned one called Hugo and one even appeared alongside Elvis on stage during a live performance of "Hound Dog".

YARN

Size A (B, C)

● 50g (50g, 50g)DK Brown

○ 10g (25g, 25g) DK White

Scrap yarn DK Black

SIZES

A: Preemie

B: Newborn – 3 months

C: 6 months – 1 year and beyond

TOOLS

4mm hook

Tapestry needle

TENSION

10 sts x 8 rows = 10cm/4in measured over treble crochet

PATTERN NOTES

The snout is crocheted in the round and then worked in rows to form the nose stripe.

BEANIE

With brown

5ch. Join with a sl st in first ch to form a ring.

Rnd 1: 3ch (counts as first tr here and throughout), 9 (11, 11)tr in ring, join - 10 (12, 12) sts.

Rnd 2: 3ch, [2tr in next st] 9 [11, 11] times, 1tr in same st as starting 3 ch, join - 20 (24, 24) sts.

Rnd 3: 3ch, [2tr in next st, 1tr] 9 [11, 11] times, 2tr in next st, join - 30 (36, 36) sts.

Rnd 4: 3ch, [2tr in next st, 2tr] 9 [11, 11] times, 2tr in next st, 1tr, join - 40 (48, 48) sts.

SIZE A & B ONLY

Rnds 5-8: 3ch, 1tr in each st around, join - 40 (48) sts.

For size A only fasten off, weave in end.

SIZE B ONLY

Rnds 9-10: 3ch, 1tr in each st around, join.

If making the hat for a baby over 2 months old, crochet one more round.

Fasten off, weave in end.

SIZE C ONLY

Rnd 5: 3ch, [2tr in next st, 3tr] 11 times, 2tr in next st, 2tr, join - 60 sts.

Rnds 6-14: 3ch, 1tr in in each st around, join.

Fasten off, weave in end.

SNOUT

With white

SIZE A ONLY

Rnd 1: Magic ring, 2ch (counts as first htr), (1htr, 3dc, 3htr, 3dc, 1htr) in ring, join - 12 sts.

Rnd 2: 2ch, 2htr in next st, 2dc in each of next 3 sts, 2htr in each of next 3 sts, 2dc in each of next 3 sts, 2htr in next st, 1htr in same st as starting 2 ch, join - 24 sts.

Rnd 3: 2ch, 2htr in next st, 1htr, [2dc in next st, 1dc] 3 times, [2htr in next st, 1htr] 3 times, [2dc in next st, 1dc] 3 times, 2htr in next st, 1htr, 2htr in next st, join - 36 sts.

Fasten off.

Skip 6 sts, rejoin yarn in next st with 1ch.

Row 1: 1dc in same st as 1 ch, 4dc. Turn - 5 sts.

Rows 2- 6: 1ch, 1dc in same st as ch, 4dc. Turn.

Fasten off.

SIZE B AND C ONLY

Rnd 1: Magic ring, 3ch (counts as first tr), (1tr, 3htr, 3tr, 3htr, 1tr) in ring, join - 12 sts.

Rnd 2: 3ch, 2tr in next st, 2htr in each of next 3 sts, 2tr in each of next 3 sts, 2htr in each of next 3 sts, 2tr in next st, 1tr in same st as starting 3 ch, join - 24 sts.

Rnd 3: 2ch (counts as 1htr), 1htr, 2htr in next st, [1dc, 2dc in next st] 3 times, [1htr, 2htr in next st] 3 times, [1dc, 2dc in next st] 3 times, 1htr, 2htr in next st, 1htr, 1htr in same st as starting 2 ch, join - 36 sts.

The next part is worked in rows.
SI st across next 7 sts.
Rows 1 -7: 1ch, 1dc in same st as ch, 4dc. Turn - 5 sts.
Fasten off for size B.

SIZE C ONLY

Rows 8-9: 1ch, 1dc in same st as ch, 4dc. Turn.

NOSE

With black

SIZE A ONLY

Rnd 1: Magic ring, 2ch, (1htr, 3dc, 3htr, 3dc, 1htr) in ring, join - 12 sts.
Fasten off. Sew onto the snout, and embroider on a smile.

SIZE B AND C ONLY

Rnd 1: Magic ring, 3ch, (1tr, 3htr, 3tr, 3htr, 1tr) in ring, join - 12 sts.
Fasten off. Sew on to the snout, and embroider on a smile.

EYES
(make 2)
With white

SIZE A ONLY

Rnd 1: Magic ring, 2ch, (1htr, 3dc, 3htr, 3dc, 1htr) in ring, join - 12 sts.
Fasten off. Use the black yarn to sew on a pupil to the whites of the eyes.

SIZE B AND C ONLY

Rnd 1: Magic ring, 3ch, work into ring 1tr, 3 (4)htr, 3 (4)tr, 3 (4)htr, 1 (2)tr, join - 12 (16) sts.
Fasten off.

PUPILS
(make 2)
With black

SIZE B AND C ONLY

Rnd 1: Magic ring, 2ch, 3htr in ring, join - 4 sts.
Fasten off and sew the pupils onto the whites of the eyes.

EARS
(make 2)
With brown

Rnd 1: Magic ring, 3ch (counts as first tr), 9 (11, 13)tr in ring, join - 10 (12, 14) sts.
Rnd 2: 3ch, 2tr in each tr around, 1tr in same st as starting 3 ch, join - 20 (24, 28) sts.
Rnds 3 - 7 (8, 11): 3ch, 1tr in each st around, join.

SIZE A ONLY

Rnd 8: 1ch, [tr2tog] 10 times, join - 10 sts.
Rnd 9: 1ch, [tr2tog] 5 times, join - 5 sts.
Fasten off. Sew onto sides of the hat.

SIZE B ONLY

Rnd 9: 3ch, [tr2tog, 1tr] 7 times, tr2tog, join - 16 sts.
Rnd 10: 1ch, [tr2tog] 8 times, join - 8 sts.
Rnd 11: [Dc2tog] 4 times, join - 4 sts.
Fasten off. Sew onto sides of the hat.

SIZE C ONLY

Rnd 12: 3ch, [tr2tog, 1tr] 9 times, join - 19 sts.
Rnd 13: 3ch, [tr2tog] 9 times, join - 10 sts.
Rnd 14: [Dc2tog] 5 times, join - 5 sts.
Fasten off. Sew onto sides of the hat.

BASSET BOOTIES

YARN

● 50g DK Brown

○ 5g DK White

Scrap yarn DK Black

SIZES

A: Newborn – 3 months
B: 3 months – 6 months
C: 6 months – 1 year

TOOLS

3.5mm hook
Tapestry needle

TENSION

9 sts x 4 rows = 6cm x 6cm
measured over treble crochet

PATTERN NOTES

The snout is not crocheted in
the round.

BOOTIES

With brown

Rnd 1: 13 (15, 17)ch, 1tr in 4th ch from hook, 1tr in each of next 8 (10, 12)ch, 6tr in last ch, working back along the other side of chain work 8 (10, 12)tr, 4tr in same st as first tr of rnd, join - 28 (32, 36) sts.

Rnd 2: 3ch (counts as first tr), 10 (12, 14)tr, 2tr in each of next 4 sts, 10 (12, 14)tr, 2tr in each of next 3 sts, 1tr in same st as starting 3 ch, join - 36 (40, 44) sts.

Rnd 3: 2ch (counts as first htr), 1htr blo in each st around, join.

Rnd 4: 2ch, 7 (9, 11)htr, [htr2tog, 1htr] 6 times, 10 (12, 14) htr, join - 30 (34, 38) sts.

Rnd 5: 2ch, 7 (9, 11)htr, [htr2tog, 1htr] 4 times, 10 (12, 14)htr, join - 26 (30, 34) sts.

Rnd 6: 2ch, 5 (7, 9)htr, [htr2tog] 6 times, 8 (10, 12)htr, join - 20 (24, 28) sts.

Rnd 7: 2ch, 7 (9, 11)htr, [htr2tog] twice, 8 (10, 12)htr, join - 18 (22, 26) sts.

SIZE A & B ONLY

Rnds 8-9: 2ch, 1htr in each st around, join - 18 (22) sts.
Fasten off.

SIZE C ONLY

Rnd 8: 2ch, 9htr, [htr2tog] 4 times, 1htr in each st to end, join - 22 sts.
Rnds 9-10: 2ch, 1htr in each st around, join.
Fasten off.

FACE

With brown
Rnd 1: Magic ring, 3ch, 9 (11, 13) tr in ring, join - 10 (12, 14) sts.
Rnd 2: 3ch, 2tr in each of next 9 (11, 13) sts, 1tr in same st as starting 3 ch, join - 20 (24, 28) sts.
Fasten off.

SNOUT

With white
Row 1: 4ch, 4tr in first ch, 4sl st along side of last tr to get to middle - 5 sts.
Rows 2-5 (5, 6): 1ch, 1dc in same st, turn - 1 st.
Fasten off. Sew onto the face.

NOSE

With black
Rnd 1: Magic ring, 1ch, 4dc in ring, join - 4 sts.
Fasten off. Sew onto the snout.

EYES

(make 2)
With white

Rnd 1: Magic ring, 1ch, 3 (4, 4)dc in ring, join - 3 (4, 4) sts.
Fasten off. Sew onto the face.
Use the black yarn to sew in pupils.

EARS

(make 2)
With brown
Rnd 1: Magic ring, 2ch (counts as first htr), 5 (7, 7)htr in ring, join - 6 (8, 8) sts.
Rnd 2: 2ch, [2htr in next st, 1htr] 2 [3, 3] times, 2htr in next st, join - 9 (12, 12) sts.
Rnds 3-6: 2ch, 1htr in each st around, join.
Rnd 7: 2ch, [htr2tog, 1htr] 2 [3, 3] times, htr2tog, join - 6 (8, 8) sts.
Fasten off. Sew onto the sides of bootie.

BUZZY BEE-NIE HAT

When you welcome a new little one into your hive it's as sweet as honey. This bright little hat was inspired by Japanese kawaii creatures.

YARN

- 25g DK Yellow
- 25g DK Black
- 10g DK White

SIZES

A: Preemie
B: Newborn – 3 months
C: 6 months – 1 year and beyond

TOOLS

4mm hook
Tapestry needle

TENSION

10 sts x 8 rows = 10cm/4in
measured over treble crochet

PATTERN NOTES

- Don't fasten off the black and yellow yarns when you make your stripes, leave them attached and pick them up for the alternative row.

- When joining rounds, work a slip stitch into top of the 3 chs at start of the round.

BEANIE

With yellow
5ch. Join with a sl st in first ch to form a ring.
Rnd 1: 3ch (counts as first tr here and throughout), 9 (11, 11)tr in ring, join - 10 (12, 12) sts.
Rnd 2: 3ch, [2tr in next st] 9 [11, 11] times, 1tr in same st as starting 3 ch, join - 20 (24, 24) sts.
Rnd 3: 3ch, [2tr in next st, 1tr] 9 [11, 11] times, 2tr in next st, join - 30 (36, 36) sts.
Rnd 4: 3ch, [2tr in next st, 2tr] 9 [11, 11] times, 2tr in next st, 1tr, join - 40 (48, 48) sts.

SIZE A AND B ONLY

With black
Rnd 5: 3ch, 1tr in each st around, join - 40 (48) sts.
With yellow
Rnd 6: 3ch, 1tr in each st around, join.
Rnds 7-8 (10): Rpt Rnds 6 & 7 once (twice) more keeping stripe

sequence correct, thus ending with a rnd worked in yellow.
If making for a child over 2 months, crochet one more round using black.
Fasten off. Weave in ends.

SIZE C ONLY

Rnd 5: 3ch, [2tr in next st, 3tr] 11 times, 2tr in next st, 2tr, join - 60 sts.

Rnd 6: 3ch, 1tr in each st around, join.
With black
Rnd 7: 1tr in each st around, join.
With yellow
Rnd 8: 1tr in each st around, join.
Rnds 9-14: Rpt rnds 6 & 7 three more times keeping striped sequence correct thus ending with a rnd worked in yellow.
Fasten off, weave in ends.

WINGS

(make 4)
With white

SIZE A AND C ONLY

Rnd 1: Magic ring, 3ch (counts as 1tr), 11tr in ring, join - 12 sts.
Rnd 2: 3ch, 2tr in each of next 11 sts, 1tr in same st as starting 3 ch, join - 24 sts.
Fasten off size A only, leaving enough yarn for sewing.

SIZE C ONLY

Rnd 3: 3ch, [2tr in next st, 1tr] 11 times, 2tr in next st, join - 36 sts.
Fasten off leaving enough yarn for sewing.

SIZE B ONLY

Rnd 1: Magic ring, 2ch (counts as 1htr), 11htr in ring, join - 12 sts.
Rnd 2: 2ch, 2htr in each of next 11 sts, 1htr in same st as starting 2 ch, join - 24 sts.
Rnd 3: 2ch, [2htr in next st, 1htr] 11 times, 2htr in next st, join - 36 sts.
Fasten off leaving enough yarn for sewing.

EYES

(make 2)
With either white or black

SIZE A ONLY

Magic ring, 1ch, 6dc in ring, join - 6 sts.
Fasten off.

SIZE B ONLY

Magic ring, 2ch, 5htr in ring, join - 6 sts.
Fasten off.

SIZE C ONLY

Magic ring, 3ch, 5tr in ring, join - 6 sts.
Fasten off.

If you have made white eyes, use a little of the black yarn to create a pupil in the middle. Sew these onto the hat.
Sew the wings onto the back of the hat, using lots of yarn so they are quite sturdy.
Embroider a little smile with either red or black yarn.

BEE BOOTIES

YARN

⬤ 25g DK Yellow

⚫ 10g DK Black

⚪ 10g DK White

SIZES

A: Newborn – 3 months
B: 3 months – 6 months
C: 6 months – 1 year

TOOLS

3.5mm hook
Tapestry needle

TENSION

9 sts x 4 rows = 6cm/2¼in
measured over treble crochet

PATTERN NOTES

- Don't fasten off the yellow and black yarns while you are creating the stripes, just form a knot.

- 3ch at the beginning of a row count as first tr, 2ch counts as first htr.

- When fastening off the wings and eyes leave enough yarn for sewing.

- The wings are the only part of the pattern not worked in the round, so you don't need to join with a slip stitch at the end of the row.

- Instructions are for one shoe so repeat the entire pattern for the second shoe.

BOOTIES

With yellow
Rnd 1: 13 (15, 17)ch, 1tr in 4th ch from hook, 1tr in each of next 8 (10, 12)ch, 6tr in last st, working back along the other side of chain work 8 (10, 12)tr, 4tr in same st as first tr of rnd, join - 28 (32, 36) sts.
Rnd 2: 3ch (counts as first tr), 10 (12, 14)tr, 2tr in each of next 4 sts, 10 (12, 14)tr, 2tr in each of next 3 sts, 1tr in same st as starting 3 ch, join - 36 (40, 44) sts.
Rnd 3: 2ch, 1htr blo in each st around, join.
With black
Rnd 4: 1ch (does not count as a st), 1dc in each st around, join.
With yellow
Rnd 5: 2ch, 7 (9, 11) htr, [htr2tog,

1htr] 5 times, 1htr in each st to end, join - 31 (35, 39) sts.
With black
Rnd 6: 1ch, 1dc in each st around, join.
With yellow
Rnd 7: 2ch, 6htr, [htr2tog] 5 [6, 8]

times, 1htr in each st to end, join - 26 (29, 31) sts.
Fasten off.
With black
Rnd 8: 1ch, 5dc, [htr2tog] 4 times, 1dc to end, join - 22 (25, 27) sts.
Fasten off.

FACE

With yellow

SIZE A AND B ONLY

Rnd 1: Magic ring, 3ch, 9 (11)tr in ring, join - 10 (12) sts.
Rnd 2: 2ch, 2htr in each of next 9 (11)sts, 1htr in same st as starting 2 ch, join - 20 (24) sts.
Fasten off.
With white, embroider on eyes, and with black, embroider on pupils and a little smile.

SIZE C ONLY

Rnd 1: Magic ring, 3ch, 11tr in ring, join - 12 sts.
Rnd 2: 3ch, 2tr in each of next 11 sts, 1tr in same st as starting 3 ch, join - 24 sts.
Fasten off.
With white, embroider on eyes, and with black, embroider on pupils and a little smile.

WINGS

(make 2)
With white

SIZE A AND B ONLY

Row 1: 8 (10)ch, 1tr in 4th ch from hook, 1tr in each of next 3 (5) ch, 6tr in last ch, 4 (6)tr, 1tr under next ch (ie bottom of 3 unworked ch at start of row) - 16 (20)tr.
Fasten off.

SIZE C ONLY

Row 1: 8ch, 1htr in 3rd ch from hook, 1htr in each of next 4 ch, 6htr in last ch, 4htr, 1htr under next ch (ie bottom of 3 unworked ch at start of row), turn - 16 sts.
Row 2: 2ch, 7htr, 2htr in each of next 3 sts, 1htr to end - 21 sts.
Fasten off.
Sew face and wings onto the bootie.

LADYBIRD HAT

Ladybirds (or ladybugs) are considered to be good luck in many cultures. I've been inspired by the more common red and black spotted ones, but they can be found in yellow, orange and brown. You could even crochet a fantastical one in purple, green or blue or with totally multicoloured spots!

YARN

Size A (B, C)

● 25g (25g, 50g) DK Red

● 10g DK Black

Scrap yarn DK White

SIZES

A: Preemie
B: Newborn – 3 months
C: 6 months – 1 year and beyond

TOOLS

4mm hook
Tapestry needle

TENSION

10 sts x 8 rows = 10cm/4in
measured over treble crochet

PATTERN NOTES

When fastening off the spots,
face and eyes, leave enough yarn
for sewing.

BEANIE

With red
5ch. Join with a sl st in first ch to form
a ring.
Rnd 1: 3ch (counts as first tr here and
throughout), 9 (11, 11)tr in ring, join -
10 (12, 12) sts.
Rnd 2: 3ch, [2tr in next st] 9 [11, 11]
times, 1tr in same st as starting 3 ch,
join - 20 (24, 24) sts.

Rnd 3: 3ch, [2tr in next st, 1tr] 9
[11, 11] times, 2tr in next st, join -
30 (36, 36) sts.
Rnd 4: 3ch, [2tr in next st, 2tr] 9
[11, 11] times, 2tr in next st, 1tr, join
- 40 (48, 48) sts.

SIZE A ONLY

Rnds 5-8: 3ch, 1tr in each st
around, join - 40 sts.
Fasten off. Weave in ends.

SIZE B ONLY

Rnds 5-10: 3ch, 1tr in each st
around, join - 48 sts.
*Fasten off. Weave in ends. If
making for a child over 2 months,
crochet an 11th round.*

SIZE C ONLY

Rnd 5: 3ch, [2tr in next st, 3tr] 11
times, 2tr in next st, 2tr, join - 60 sts.
Rnds 6-14: 3ch, 1tr in each st
around, join.
Fasten off.

FACE

With black
Rnd 1: 4ch, 9tr in first ch, join - 10 sts.
Rnd 2: 3ch, 2tr in each st around, 1tr in same st as 3ch, join - 20 sts.
For size A, fasten off and leave enough yarn for sewing and embroidering on antennae.

SIZE B AND C ONLY

Rnd 3: 3ch, 2tr in each st around, 1tr in same st as 3ch, join - 40 sts.
Fasten off and leave enough yarn for sewing.

EYES

(make 2)
With white

SIZE A ONLY

Rnd 1: 2ch, 5dc in first ch, join - 6 sts.
Fasten off and leave enough yarn for sewing.

SIZE B AND C ONLY

Rnd 1: 3ch, 5 (9)htr in first st, join - 6 (10) sts.
Fasten off and leave enough yarn for sewing.

SPOTS

I've recommended a number of spots but you may decide to do more or fewer depending on how you'd like your finished ladybird to be. Leave enough yarn for sewing.

SIZE A ONLY

(make 8)
With black
Rnd 1: 3ch, 7htr in first ch, join - 8 sts.
Fasten off and leave enough yarn for sewing.

SIZE B AND C

(make 10-14)
With black
Rnd 1: 4ch, 7tr (9) in first ch from hook, join to 4th ch - 8 (10) sts.
Fasten off and leave enough yarn for sewing.

Sew the eyes onto the face. Use a small amount of black yarn to embroider on pupils.

With a small amount of the red yarn to embroider on a mouth, use the lines in between rows as a guide to make a smile.

Sew the face onto the hat and embroider two antennae.

Sew the spots all around the hat. Weave in any loose ends.

LADYBIRD BOOTIES

YARN

● 25g (50g for size C) DK Red

● 10g DK Black

Scrap yarn DK white

SIZES

A: Newborn – 3 months
B: 3 months – 6 months
C: 6 months – 1 year

TOOLS

3.5mm hook
Tapestry needle

TENSION

9 sts x 4 rows = 6cm/2¼in measured over treble crochet

PATTERN NOTES

· 3ch at the start of a round counts as 1tr

· 2ch at the start of a round counts as 1htr

BOOTIES

With red

Rnd 1: 13 (15, 17)ch, 1tr in 4th ch from hook, 1tr in each of next 8 (10, 12)ch, 6tr in last ch, working back along the other side of chain work 8 (10, 12)tr, 4tr in same st as first tr of rnd, join - 28 (32, 36) sts.

Rnd 2: 3ch (counts as first tr), 10 (12, 14)tr, 2tr in each of next 4 sts, 10 (12, 14)tr, 2tr in each of next 3 sts, 1tr in same st as starting 3 ch, join - 36 (40, 44) sts.

Rnd 3: 2ch (counts as first htr), 1htr blo in each st around, join.

Rnd 4: 2ch, 7 (9, 11) htr, [htr2tog, 1htr] 6 times, 10 (12, 14) htr, join - 30 (34, 38) sts.

Rnd 5: 2ch, 7 (9, 11)htr, [htr2tog, 1htr] 4 times, 10 (12, 14)htr, join - 26 (30, 34) sts.

Rnd 6: 2ch, 5 (7, 9)htr, [htr2tog] 6 times, 8 (10, 12)htr, join - 20 (24, 28) sts.

SIZE A AND B ONLY

Rnd 7: 1ch, 7 (9)dc, [htr2tog] twice, 1dc in each st to end, join - 18 (22) sts.

Fasten off. Weave in ends.

SIZE C ONLY

Rnd 7: 1ch, 9dc, [tr2tog] 4 times, 1dc in each st to end, join - 24 sts.

Rnd 8: 1ch, 10dc, htr2tog, 1dc to end, join - 23 sts.

FACE

With black

SIZE A ONLY

Rnd 1: 4ch, 9tr in first ch, join with a sl st to 4th ch - 10 sts.
Rnd 2: 2ch, 2htr in each st around, 1htr in same st as 2ch, join - 20 sts.
Fasten off. Leave a long tail for sewing.

SIZE B AND C ONLY

Rnd 1: 4ch, 11 (13)tr in first ch, join - 12 (14) sts.
Rnd 2: 3ch, 2tr in each st around, 1tr in same st as 3ch, join - 24 (28) sts.
Fasten off. Leave a long tail for sewing.

EYES

(make 2)
With white

SIZE A & B ONLY

Rnd 1: 2ch, 4 (6)dc in first ch, join - 4 (6) sts.
Fasten off, leave enough yarn for sewing and sew them onto the face.

SIZE C ONLY

Rnd 1: 3ch, 5htr in first ch, join to 3rd ch - 6 sts.
Fasten off, leave enough yarn for sewing and sew them onto the face.

Use the black yarn to create little pupils on the eyes.

Use a little red yarn to embroider on a smile. Sew the face onto the front of the shoe.

SPOTS

(make 7)

SIZE A & B ONLY

Rnd 1: 2ch, 4 (6)dc in first ch, join to 2nd ch - 4 (6) sts.
Fasten off, leave enough yarn for sewing. Sew three on each side, and one at the back.

SIZE C ONLY

Rnd 1: 3ch, 5htr in first ch, join to 3rd ch - 6 sts.
Fasten off, leave enough yarn for sewing. Sew three on each side, and one at the back.

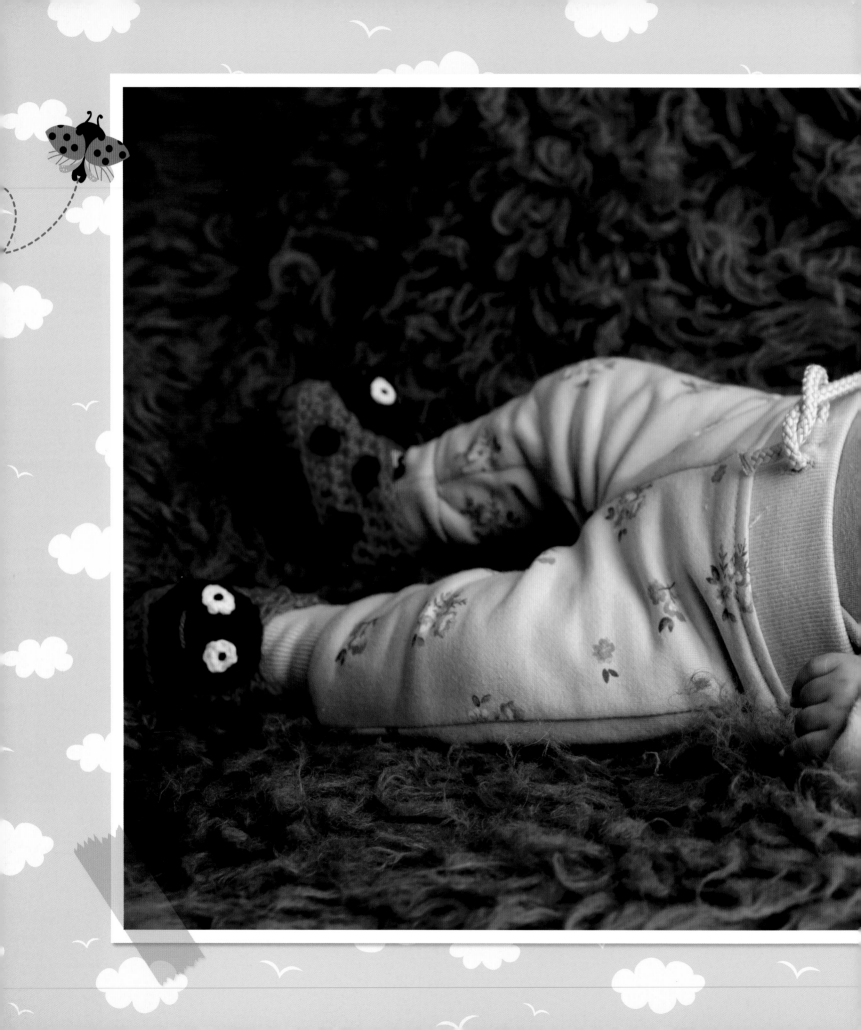

GIRAFFE BEANIE HAT

Giraffes have the biggest hearts of all land mammals. I like to name my creations as I go along, and I called this one Jessye (with a y!) after a friend who has a very big heart.

YARN

Size A (B, C)

 25g (25g, 50g) DK Yellow

● 10g DK Light Brown

Scrap yarn DK White
Scrap yarn DK Black

SIZES

A: Preemie
B: Newborn – 3 months
C: 6 months – 1 year and beyond

TOOLS

4mm hook
Tapestry needle

TENSION

10 sts x 8 rows = 10cm/4in measured over treble crochet

PATTERN NOTES

· 3ch at the beginning of a row counts as 1tr.

· 2ch at the beginning of a row counts as 1htr.

· Apart from the snout, everything in this pattern is crocheted in the round, at the end of every row slip stitch to the top chain from start of the round.

· When you've fastened off the horns (known as ossicones), ears, eyes and snout, leave enough yarn for sewing.

BEANIE

With yellow

5ch. Join with a sl st in first ch to form a ring.

Rnd 1: 3ch (counts as first tr here and throughout), 9 (11, 11)tr in ring, join - 10 (12, 12) sts.

Rnd 2: 3ch, [2tr in next st] 9 [11, 11] times, 1tr in same st as starting 3 ch, join - 20 (24, 24) sts.

Rnd 3: 3ch, [2tr in next st, 1tr] 9 [11, 11] times, 2tr in next st, join - 30 (36, 36) sts.

Rnd 4: 3ch, [2tr in next st, 2tr] 9 [11, 11] times, 2tr in next st, 1tr, join - 40 (48, 48) sts.

SIZE A & B ONLY

Rnds 5-8: 3ch, 1tr in each st around, join - 40 (48) sts.
Size A only fasten off.

SIZE B ONLY

Rnds 9-10: 3ch, 1tr in each st around, join.
If making the hat for a baby over 2 months, crochet an 11th round of trebles.
Fasten off.

SIZE C ONLY

Rnd 5: 3ch, [2tr in next st, 3tr] 11 times, 2tr in next st, 2tr, join - 60 sts.
Rnds 6-14: 3ch, 1tr in each st around, join.
Fasten off, weave in end.

EYES

(make 2)
With white
Rnd 1: 4ch, 7 (9, 15)tr in first ch, join with sl st to 4th ch- 8 (10, 16) sts.
Fasten off.

PUPILS

(make 2)
With black

SIZE A ONLY

Rnd 1: 2ch, 3dc in first ch, join with sl st to 2nd ch - 4 sts.

SIZE B AND C ONLY

Magic ring. Rnd 1: 3ch, 3 (5)htr in ring, join with sl st to 3rd ch - 4 (6) sts.
Fasten off.
Sew the pupils onto the whites of the eyes.

SNOUT

With light brown
Worked in rows, turn at the end of each row.

SIZE A ONLY

Row 1: 3ch, 5htr in first ch. Turn - 6 sts.
Row 2: 2ch, 1htr in same st as 2ch, 2htr in each of next 5 sts. Turn - 12 sts.
Row 3: 2ch, [2htr in next st, 1htr] 5 times, 2htr in last st. Turn - 18 sts.
Row 4: 2ch, [2htr in next st, 2htr] 5 times, 2htr in next st, 1htr - 24 sts.
Fasten off.

SIZE B & C ONLY

Row 1: 4ch, 5 (7)tr in first ch. Turn - 6 (8) sts.
Row 2: 3ch, 1tr in same st as 3ch, 2tr in each of rem 5 (7) sts. Turn - 12 (16) sts.
Row 3: 3ch, [2tr in next st, 1tr] 5 [7] times, 2tr in last st. Turn - 18 (24) sts.

Row 4: 3ch, [2tr in next st, 2tr] 5 [7] times, 2tr in next st, 1tr - 24 (32) sts.
Fasten off.

EARS

(make 2)
With yellow

SIZE A ONLY

Rnd 1: 3ch, 7htr in first ch, join with sl st to 3rd ch - 8 sts.
Rnd 2: 2ch, 2htr in each st around, 1htr in same st as starting 2 ch, join - 16 sts.
Rnd 3: 2ch, 1htr in each st around, join.
Rnd 4: 2ch, [htr2tog, 1htr] 5 times, join - 11 sts.
Fasten off.

SIZE B AND C ONLY

Rnd 1: 4ch, 7 (9)tr in first ch, join - 8 (10) sts.

Rnd 2: 3ch, 2tr in each st around, 1tr in same st as starting 3 ch, join - 16 (20) sts.
Rnd 3: 3ch, 1tr in each st around, join.

SIZE B ONLY

Rnd 4: 3ch, [tr2tog, 1tr] 5 times, join - 11 sts.
Fasten off.

SIZE C ONLY

Rnd 4: 3ch, [tr2tog, 1tr] 6 times, 1tr, join - 14 sts.
Fasten off.

HORNS
(make 2)

SIZE A ONLY

With light brown
Rnd 1: 3ch, 9htr in first ch, join with sl st to 3rd ch - 10 sts.
Rnd 2: 2ch, 1htr in each st around, join.
Fasten off.
With yellow
Rnds 3-4: 2ch, 1htr in each st around, join.
Fasten off.

SIZES B & C ONLY

With light brown
Rnd 1: 4ch, 9 (11)tr in first ch, join with sl st to 4th ch - 10 (12) sts.
Rnd 2: 3ch, 1tr in each st around, join.
Fasten off.
With yellow
Rnds 3-4: 3ch, 1tr in each st around, join.
Fasten off.

Sew the snout, horns, eyes and ears onto the hat using the picture as your guide. Make sure the hat's seam is at the back in the middle. Weave in any ends that are loose.

GIRAFFE BOOTIES

YARN

 25g DK Yellow

● 10g DK Light Brown

Scrap yarn DK White
Scrap yarn DK Black
Scrap yarn DK Dark Brown
(optional, light brown can be
used in place of dark brown)

SIZES

A: Newborn – 3 months
B: 3 months – 6 months
C: 6 months – 1 year

TOOLS

3.5mm hook
Tapestry needle

TENSION

9 sts x 4 rows = 6cm/2¼in
measured over treble
crochet

PATTERN NOTES

- 3ch at the start of a row
  counts as 1tr.

- 2ch at the start of a row
  counts as 1htr.

BOOTIE

With yellow
Rnd 1: 13 (15, 17)ch, 1tr in 4th ch from hook, 1tr in each of next 8 (10, 12)ch, 6tr in last ch, working back along the other side of chain work 8 (10, 12)tr, 4tr in same st as first tr of rnd, join - 28 (32, 36) sts.
Rnd 2: 3ch (counts as first tr), 10 (12, 14)tr, 2tr in each of next 4 sts, 10 (12, 14)tr, 2tr in each of next 3 sts, 1tr in same st as starting 3 ch, join - 36 (40, 44) sts.
Rnd 3: 2ch (counts as first htr), 1htr blo in each st around, join.
Rnd 4: 2ch, 7 (9, 11) htr, [htr2tog, 1htr] 6 times, 10 (12, 14) htr, join - 30 (34, 38) sts.
Rnd 5: 2ch, 7 (9, 11)htr, [htr2tog, 1htr] 4 times, 10 (12, 14)htr, join - 26 (30, 34) sts.
Rnd 6: 2ch, 5 (7, 9)htr, [htr2tog] 6 times, 8 (10, 12)htr, join - 20 (24, 28) sts.
Rnd 7: 2ch, 7 (9, 11)htr, [htr2tog] twice, 8 (10, 12)htr, join - 18 (22, 26) sts.

SIZE A & B ONLY

Rnds 8-9: 2ch, 1htr in each st around, join - 18 (22) sts.
Fasten off.

SIZE C ONLY

Rnd 8: 2ch, 9htr, [htr2tog] 4 times, 1htr in each st to end, join - 22 sts.
Rnds 9-10: 2ch, 1htr in each st around, join.
Fasten off.

EARS

(make 2)

With yellow

Rnd 1: Magic ring, 3ch, 5 (7, 9)tr in ring, join - 6 (8, 10) sts.

Fasten off.

SNOUT

With light brown

Rnd 1: 7 (8, 9)ch, 1htr in 3rd ch from hook, 1htr in each of next 3 (4, 5) ch, 4htr in last ch, working along the back of the ch work 3 (4, 5)htr, 2htr in final st, join - 14 (16, 18)htr.

Rnd 2: 2ch, 2htr in same st, 4 (5, 6)htr, 2htr in each of next 3 sts, 4 (5, 6)htr, 2htr in next st, 1htr in same st as starting 2 ch, join - 20 (22, 24)sts.

Fasten off.

SPOTS

(make between 3-5)

With light or dark brown

SIZE A AND B ONLY

Rnd 1: Magic ring, 6dc in ring, join - 6 sts.

Fasten off.

SIZE C ONLY

Rnd 1: Magic ring, 2ch, 5htr in ring, join - 6 sts.

Fasten off.

HORNS

(officially called ossicones!)

(make 2)

SIZE A AND B ONLY

With light or dark brown

Rnd 1: Magic ring, 2ch, 5 (6)htr in ring, join - 6 (7) sts.

Fasten off.

With yellow

Rnds 2-3: 2ch, 5 (6)htr, join.

Fasten off.

SIZE C ONLY

With light or dark brown

Rnd 1: Magic ring, 3ch, 5tr in ring, join - 6 sts.

Fasten off.

With yellow

Rnds 2-3: 3ch, 5tr, join.

Fasten off.

EYES

(make 2)

With white

Rnd 1: Magic ring, 6 (6, 8)dc in ring, join - 6 (6, 8) sts.

Fasten off.

Use a little black (or dark brown) to make a small pupil.

Sew the eyes, ears, horns, snout and spots onto the bootie. Weave in all ends.

MONSTER HAT

You can use the elements in this pattern to create whatever type of monster you like, as many eyes, horns, teeth etc as you fancy. This might be a fun project for an older sibling to help design the kind of monster they want to create.

YARN

Size A (B, C)

 25g (25g, 50g)
DK Green (see pattern notes)

◯ 25g DK White

● 10g DK Blue

Scrap yarn DK Black
Scrap DK yarn in other colours for spots (optional)

OTHER MATERIALS

Small amount of toy stuffing (optional if making horns – see pattern notes)

TOOLS

4mm hook
Tapestry needle

TENSION

10 sts x 8 rows = 10cm/4in measured over treble crochet

PATTERN NOTES

- This hat would lend itself well to a furry/eyelash yarn eg Sirdar Funky Fur, as it will give the hat a furry feeling. If you've never used this type of yarn before it may be worth creating a few squares to get used to it beforehand.

- I haven't included quantities for the teeth, horns, eyes, spots and spikes so you can get creative and your monster will be completely unique.

- The horns don't need to be stuffed, but you may want give them a stronger structure. See page 8.

BEANIE

With green
5ch. Join with a sl st in first ch to form a ring.
Rnd 1: 3ch (counts as first tr here and throughout), 9 (11, 11)tr in ring, join - 10 (12, 12) sts.
Rnd 2: 3ch, [2tr in next st] 9 [11, 11] times, 1tr in same st as starting 3 ch, join - 20 (24, 24) sts.
Rnd 3: 3ch, [2tr in next st, 1tr] 9 [11, 11] times, 2tr in next st, join - 30 (36, 36) sts.
Rnd 4: 3ch, [2tr in next st, 2tr] 9 [11, 11] times, 2tr in next st, 1tr, join - 40 (48, 48) sts.

SIZE A & B ONLY

Rnds 5-8: 3ch, 1tr in each st around, join - 40 (48) sts.
Size A only fasten off, weave in end.

SIZE B ONLY

Rnds 9-10: 3ch, 1tr in each st around, join.
If making the hat for a baby over 2 months, crochet an 11th round of trebles.
Fasten off, weave in end.

SIZE C ONLY

Rnd 5: 3ch, [2tr in next st, 3tr] 11 times, 2tr in next st, 2tr, join - 60 sts.
Rnds 6-14: 3ch, 1tr in each st around, join.
Fasten off, weave in end.

SPIKE

With blue

Rnd 1: Magic ring, 2ch, 3htr in ring, join - 4 sts.
Rnd 2: 2ch, 2htr in next st, 1htr, 2htr in next st, join - 6 sts.
Rnd 3: 2ch, 2htr in next st, [1htr, 2htr in next st] twice, join - 9 sts.
Fasten off, weave in end.

HORN

With white

Rnd 1: Magic ring, 2ch, 3htr in ring, join - 4 sts.
Rnd 2: 2ch, 2htr in next st, 1htr, 2htr in next st, join - 6 sts.
Rnd 3: 2ch, 2htr in next st, [1htr, 2htr in next st] twice, join - 9 sts.
Rnds 4-5: 2ch, 1htr in each st around, join.
If you'd like it to be longer, repeat Rnd 4 as many times as you like. You may want to stuff it to give it some structure.

EYES

With white

Rnd 1: Magic ring, 3ch, 7tr in ring, join - 8 sts.
For eyes that will have a 2.5cm/1in diameter, fasten off here.
For eyes that will have a 4.5cm/1¾in diameter, continue to Rnd 2.
Rnd 2: 2ch, 2htr in each of next 7 sts, 1htr in same st as 2ch, join - 16 sts.
Fasten off, leaving enough yarn for sewing.

PUPILS

With black

Magic ring, 4dc in ring, join - 4 sts.
Fasten off. Sew onto the main eye.

TEETH

With white

Row 1: 4ch, sl st in 2nd ch from hook, 1htr in next ch, 1tr next ch - 3 sts.
Fasten off, weave in end.

EARS

With green

SIZE A ONLY

Rnd 1: Magic ring, 2ch, 5htr in ring, join - 6 sts.
Rnd 2: 2ch, 2htr in each of next 5 sts, 1htr in same st as 2ch, join - 12 sts.

Rnd 3: 2ch [2htr in next st, 1htr] 5 times, 2htr in last st, join - 18 sts.
Rnds 4-6: 2ch, 1htr in each st around, join.
Fasten off.
Fold the ear and sew onto the sides of the hat.

SIZE B AND C ONLY

Rnd 1: Magic ring, 3ch, 5tr in ring, join - 6 sts.
Rnd 2: 3ch, 2tr in each of next 5 sts, 1tr in same st as 3ch, join - 12 sts.
Rnd 3: 3ch [2tr in next st, 1tr] 5 times, 2tr in last st, join - 18 sts.
Rnds 4-6: 3ch, 1tr in each st around, join.
Fasten off.
Fold the ear and sew onto the sides of the hat.

SMALL NOSE

With green
(This will be an oval shape with a width of 3cm/1¼in along the middle)
Row 1: Magic ring, 2ch, (2htr, 3tr, 3htr, 3tr) in ring, join - 12 sts.
Row 2: 2ch, 1htr in each st around, join.
Fasten off. Sew nose onto the front of the hat.

BIG NOSE

With green
(This will be an oval shape with a width of 5cm/2in along the middle)
Row 1: Magic ring, 2ch, (2htr, 3tr, 3htr, 3tr) in ring, join - 12 sts.
Row 2: 2ch, [2htr in next st, 1htr] 5 times, 2htr in next st, join - 18 sts.
Row 3: 2ch, 1htr in each st around, join.
Fasten off. Sew nose onto the front of the hat.

Optional – sew on a wart with some scrap yarn.

SPOTS

SIZE A ONLY

Rnd 1: Magic ring, 6dc in ring, join - 6 sts.
Fasten off.

SIZE B ONLY

Rnd 1: Magic ring, 2ch, 5htr in ring, join - 6 sts.
Fasten off.

SIZE C ONLY

Rnd 1: Magic ring, 3ch, 6tr in ring, join - 6 sts.
Fasten off.

MONSTER FEET

YARN

 25g DK Green

Scrap yarn DK Blue

SIZES
A: Newborn – 3 months
B: 3 months – 6 months
C: 6 months – 1 year

TOOLS
3.5mm hook
Tapestry needle

TENSION
9 sts x 4 rows = 6cm/2¼in
measured over treble crochet

PATTERN NOTES
- Make the nails before starting on the feet.
- Cut off around 50cm/19¾in of yarn of the main colour before you begin the shoes.

BOOTIES

NAILS
(make 4)
With blue
Rnd 1: Magic ring, (2dc, 1htr, 1tr, 1htr, 2dc) in ring, join - 7 sts.
Fasten off.

FEET
With green
Rnd 1: 13 (15, 17)ch, 1tr in 4th ch from hook, 1tr in each of next 8 (10, 12)ch, 6tr in last ch, working back along the other side of chain work 8 (10, 12)tr, 4tr in same st as first tr of rnd, join - 28 (32, 36) sts.

Rnd 2: 3ch, 10 (12, 14)tr, 2tr in each of next 4 sts, 10 (12, 14)tr, 2tr in each of next 3 sts, 1tr in same st as starting 3 ch, join - 36 (40, 44) sts.
Rnd 3: 1ch, 1dc blo in same st as 1ch, 10 (12, 14)dc blo, 2tr blo in each of next 8 sts, 1dc blo in each st to end, join - 44 (48, 52) sts.
Rnd 4: 1ch, 1dc in same st as 1ch, 10 (12, 14)dc, [tr2tog] 8 times, 1dc in each st to end, join - 36 (40, 44) sts.
Rnd 5: 1ch, 1dc in same st as 1ch, 10 (12, 14)dc, [tr2tog] 4 times, 1dc in each st to end, join - 32 (36, 40) sts.
Rnd 6: 1ch, 1dc in same st as 1ch, 10 (12, 14)dc, [tr2tog] twice, 1dc in

each st to end, join - 30 (34, 38) sts.

Sew on the blue nails to the front of the shoe (rnd 4) evenly spaced.

Using the 50cm/20in of yarn to create definition between the toes between the increases of Rnd 3 and decreases of Rnd 4, being careful not to sew onto the soles (Rnds 1-2).

Rnd 7: 2ch, 7 (9, 11)htr, [htr2tog] 4 times, 1htr in each st to end, join - 26 (30, 34) sts.

Rnd 8: 2ch, 6 (8, 10)htr, [htr2tog] 4 times, 1htr in each st to end, join - 22 (26, 30) sts.

Rnd 9: 2ch, 6 (8, 10)htr, [htr2tog] twice, 1htr in each st to end, join - 20 (24, 28) sts.

Optional

Rnd 10: 2ch, 1htr in each st around, join.

Fasten off.

SHARK BEANIE

Which tune sticks in your head more: the Jaws theme or Baby Shark? These underwater predators have been around for over 420 million years – so they are older than dinosaurs!

YARN

Size A (B, C)

⬤ 25g (25g, 50g) DK Blue

◯ 10g DK White

Scrap yarn DK Black
Scrap yarn DK Red

SIZES

A: Preemie
B: Newborn – 3 months
C: 6 months – 1 year and beyond

TOOLS

4mm hook
Tapestry needle

TENSION

10 sts x 8 rows = 10cm/4in
measured over treble crochet

PATTERN NOTES

You may want to add an extra fin
at the back for older babies.

BEANIE

With blue
5ch. Join with a sl st in first ch to
form a ring.
Rnd 1: 3ch (counts as first tr here
and throughout), 9 (11, 11)tr in
ring, join - 10 (12, 12) sts.
Rnd 2: 3ch, [2tr in next st] 9 [11, 11]
times, 1tr in same st as starting 3
ch, join - 20 (24, 24) sts.
Rnd 3: 3ch, [2tr in next st, 1tr] 9
[11, 11] times, 2tr in next st, join -
30 (36, 36) sts.
Rnd 4: 3ch, [2tr in next st, 2tr] 9
[11, 11] times, 2tr in next st, 1tr, join
- 40 (48, 48) sts.

SIZE A & B ONLY

Rnds 5-8: 3ch, 1tr in each st
around, join.
For size A only fasten off.

SIZE B ONLY

Rnds 9-10: 3ch, 1tr in each st
around join.
*If making the hat for a baby
over 2 months, crochet an 11th
round of trebles.
Fasten off.*

SIZE C ONLY

Rnd 5: 3ch, [2tr in next st, 3tr] 11

times, 2tr in next st, 2tr, join -
60 sts.
Rnds 6-14: 3ch, 1tr in each st
around, join.
Fasten off, weave in end.

TEETH

With red
Row 1: 14 (18, 22)ch, 1dc in 2nd ch
from hook and in each ch to end

- 13 (17, 21) sts.
*Fasten off.
Instead of turning, start on the
right-hand side.
With white*
Row 2: Rejoin yarn in first st,
*4ch, 1dc in 2nd ch from hook,
1htr in next ch, 1tr in next ch, miss
next 3 sts of Row 1, sl st in next st;
rpt from * a further 2 (3, 4) times.
Fasten off.

EYES

(make 2)
With white
Size A only
Rnd 1: Magic ring, 3ch, 9tr in ring, join - 10 sts.
Fasten off.

SIZE B ONLY

Rnd 1: Magic ring, 2ch, 5htr in ring, join - 6 sts.
Rnd 2: 3ch, [2tr in next st] 5 times, 1tr in same st as starting 3ch, join - 12 sts.
Fasten off.

SIZE C ONLY

Rnd 1: Magic ring, 3ch, 7tr in ring, join - 8 sts.
Rnd 2: 2ch, [2htr in next st] 7 times, 1htr in same st as starting 2ch, join - 16 sts.
Fasten off.

PUPILS

(make 2)
With black

SIZE A ONLY

Rnd 1: Magic ring, 4dc in ring, join - 4 sts.
Fasten off. Sew onto eyes.

SIZE B & C ONLY

Rnd 1: Magic ring, 2ch, 5htr in ring, join - 6 sts.
Fasten off. Sew onto eyes.

DORSAL FIN

With blue
All sizes start in the same way
Rnd 1: Magic ring, 3ch, 5tr in ring, join - 6 sts.
Rnd 2: 3ch, [2tr in next st] 4 times, 1tr, join - 10 sts.
Rnd 3: 3ch, 1tr, [2tr in next st] 6

times, 2tr, join - 16 sts.
For size A, fasten off, sew to the top of the hat.

SIZE B ONLY

Rnd 4: 3ch, 3tr, [2tr in next st, 1tr] 4 times, 4tr, join - 20 sts.
Rnd 5: 3ch, 3tr, [2tr in next st, 2tr] 4 times, 4tr, join - 24 sts.
Fasten off, sew to the top of the hat.

SIZE C ONLY

Rnd 4: 3ch, 3tr, 2tr in next st, 1tr, [2tr in next st] 4 times, 1tr, 2tr in next st, 4tr, join - 22 sts.
Rnd 5: 3ch, 8tr, [2tr in next st] 4 times, 9tr, join - 26 sts.
Rnd 6: 3ch, 1tr in each st around, join.
Fasten off, sew to the top of the hat.

SIDE FINS

(make 2)
With blue
The first two rounds are the same for each size.
Rnd 1: Magic ring, 3ch, 5tr in ring, join - 6 sts.
Rnd 2: 3ch, [2tr in next st] 5 times, 1tr in same st as starting 3ch, join - 12 sts.

SIZE A ONLY

Rnd 3: 3ch, [2tr in next st, 2tr] 3 times, 2tr in next st, 1tr, join - 16 sts.
Fasten off, sew to the sides.

SIZE B ONLY

Rnd 3: 3ch, [2tr in next st, 1tr] 5 times, 2tr in next st, join - 18 sts.
Rnds 4-5: 3ch, 1tr in each st around, join.
Fasten off, sew to the sides.

SIZE C ONLY

Rnd 3: 3ch, [2tr in next st, 1tr] 5 times, 2tr in next st, join - 18 sts.
Rnd 4: 3ch, [2tr in next st, 2tr] 5 times, 2tr in next st, 1tr, join - 24 sts.
Rnds 5-6: 3ch, 1tr in each st around, join.
Fasten off, sew to sides.

To fin-ish off (sorry!) sew the eyes and teeth onto the shark. Use the black yarn to sew on two nostrils (optional). Weave in any loose ends.

SHARK BOOTIES

YARN

 25g DK Blue

⚪ 10g DK White

Scrap yarn DK Red
Scrap yarn DK Black (optional)

SIZES

A: Newborn – 3 months
B: 3 months – 6 months
C: 6 months – 1 year

TOOLS

3.5mm hook
Tapestry needle

TENSION

9 sts x 4 rows = 6cm/2¼in
measured over treble crochet

PATTERN NOTES

• If you're making size C, you
  may need to a familiarise
  yourself with the double
  treble crochet stitch (dtr).

• If you don't have black yarn
  to hand you can use the blue
  yarn.

BOOTIES

With blue
Rnd 1: 13 (15, 17)ch, 1tr in 4th ch
from hook, 1tr in each of next 8
(10, 12)ch, 6tr in last ch, working
back along the other side of chain
work 8 (10, 12)tr, 4tr in same st as
first tr of rnd, join - 28 (32, 36) sts.
Rnd 2: 3ch, 10 (12, 14)tr, 2tr in
each of next 4 sts, 10 (12, 14)tr, 2tr
in each of next 3 sts, 1tr in same
st as starting 3 ch, join - 36 (40,
44) sts.
Rnd 3: 1ch, 1dc blo in each st
around, join.
Rnd 4: 1ch, 6 (8, 10)dc, fasten off
blue, with white yarn 16 (18, 20)
dc, fasten off white, with blue
yarn 1dc in each st to end, join.
Rnds 5-6: 1ch, 1dc in each st
around, join.
Use the red yarn to embroider a
line above the white teeth.
Rnd 7: 1ch, 5 (7, 9)dc, [dc2tog] 8
times, 1dc in each st to end, join -
28 (32, 36) sts.
Rnd 8: 1ch, 4 (6, 8)dc, [htr2tog] 4
times, 1dc in each st to end, join -
24 (28, 32) sts.
Rnd 9: 1ch, 4 (6, 8)dc, [htr2tog]
twice, 1dc in each st to end, join -
22 (26, 30) sts.
Rnd 10: 1ch, 3 (5, 7)dc, [htr2tog]
twice, 1dc in each st to end, join -
20 (24, 28) sts.

SIZE A ONLY

Rnds 11 - 15: 1ch, 1dc in each st
around, join.
Fasten off, weave in ends.

SIZE B & C ONLY

Rnds 11 - 18: 1ch, 1dc in each st
around, join.
Fasten off, weave in ends.

EYES

(make 2)

With white

Rnd 1: Magic ring, 4 (6, 6)dc in ring, join - 4 (6, 6) sts.

Use the black or blue yarn to make a small pupil in the middle.

FINS

(make 4)

With blue

Start your slip knot at 10cm/4in into the yarn. These are not made in the round.

SIZE A ONLY

Row 1: 5ch, 1dc in 2nd ch from hook, 1htr in next ch, 1tr in each of next 2 ch - 4 sts.

Fasten off.

SIZE B ONLY

Row 1: 6ch, 1dc in 2nd ch from hook, 1htr in each of next 2 ch, 1tr in each of next 2 ch - 5 sts.

Fasten off.

SIZE C ONLY

Row 1: 7ch, 1dc in 2nd ch from hook, 1htr in next ch, 1tr in next ch, 1dtr in each of next 3 ch - 6 sts.

Fasten off.

Sew two together to make the dorsal fin and sew this on the front. Sew the other two onto each side of the shark.

TIGER BEANIE

Crochet up this grrrrreat hat for the little tiger cub in your life.
You can also use the same pattern to create a little teddy bear hat.

YARN

Size A (B, C)

⬤ 25g (25g, 50g) DK Orange

⬤ 25g DK Black

◯ 10g DK White

⬤ 5g DK Yellow (optional)

SIZES

A: Preemie
B: Newborn – 3 months
C: 6 months – 1 year and beyond

TOOLS

4mm hook
Tapestry needle

TENSION

10 sts x 8 rows = 10cm/4in measured over treble crochet

PATTERN NOTES

You can use this pattern to make a teddy bear as well. Just make it with brown yarn as the main colour and omit the stripes. Use white yarn for the eyes instead of yellow.

BEANIE

With orange

5ch. Join with a sl st in first ch to form a ring.
Rnd 1: 3ch (counts as first tr here and throughout), 9 (11, 11)tr in ring, join - 10 (12, 12) sts.
Rnd 2: 3ch, [2tr in next st] 9 [11, 11] times, 1tr in same st as starting 3 ch, join - 20 (24, 24) sts.
Rnd 3: 3ch, [2tr in next st, 1tr] 9 [11, 11] times, 2tr in next st, join - 30 (36, 36) sts.
Rnd 4: 3ch, [2tr in next st, 2tr] 9 [11, 11] times, 2tr in next st, 1tr, join - 40 (48, 48) sts.

SIZE A AND B ONLY

Rnds 5-8: 3ch, 1tr in each st to end, join.
For size A fasten off.

SIZE B ONLY

Rnds 9-10: 3ch, 1tr in each st to end, join. (48)
If making the hat for a baby over 2 months, crochet an 11th round of trebles.
Fasten off.

SIZE C ONLY

Rnd 5: 3ch, [2tr in next st, 3tr] 11 times, 2tr in next st, 2tr, join - 60 sts.
Rnds 6-14: 3ch, 1tr in each st to end, join.

EARS

(make 2)
With orange

SIZE A ONLY

Rnd 1: 4ch, 9tr in first ch, join - 10 sts.
Rnd 2: 3ch, [2tr in next st, 1tr] 4 times, 2tr in next st, join - 15 sts.
Rnd 3: 3ch, 1tr in each st to end, join.
Fasten off.

SIZE B ONLY

Rnd 1: 4ch, 7tr in first ch, join - 8 sts.
Rnd 2: 3ch, [2tr in next st] 7 times, 1tr in same st as 3ch, join - 16 sts.
Rnd 3: 3ch, 1tr in each st to end, join.
Fasten off.

SIZE C ONLY

Rnd 1: 4ch, 9tr in first ch, join - 10 sts.
Rnd 2: 3ch, [2tr in next st] 9 times, 1tr in same st as 3ch, join - 20 sts.

Rnds 3-4: 3ch, 1tr in each st to end, join.
Fasten off.

EYES

(make 2)
With yellow
Rnd 1: 4ch, 7 (9, 15)tr in first ch, join - 8 (10, 16) sts.
Fasten off.

SIZE A ONLY

With black
Rnd 1: 2ch, 3dc in first ch, join - 4 sts.)
Fasten off.

SIZE B AND C

With black
Rnd 1: 3ch, 3 (5)htr in first ch, join - 4 (6) sts.
Fasten off.
Sew the black circles onto the yellow circles.

SNOUT

With white
Rnd 1: 4ch, 9 (11, 9)tr in first ch, join - 10 (12, 10) sts.
Rnd 2: 3ch, [2tr in next st] 9 [11, 9] times, 1tr in same st as 3ch, join - 20 (24, 20) sts.
Fasten off size A and B

SIZE C ONLY

Rnd 3: 3ch, [2tr in next st] 19 times, 1tr in same st as 3ch, join - 40 sts.
Fasten off.

NOSE

With black

SIZE A AND B

Rnd 1: 3ch, 5 (7)htr in first ch, join - 6 (8) sts
Fasten off.
Leave enough yarn for sewing and to embroider on the mouth.

SIZE C ONLY

Rnd 1: 4ch, 9tr in first ch, join - 10 sts.
Fasten off. Leave enough yarn for sewing and to embroider on the mouth.

STRIPES

With black
(make 6 or 8 for size C)
Row 1: 14 (16, 20)ch, 1dc in 2nd ch from hook, 10 (12, 16)htr, 1dc, 1sl st - 13 (15, 19) sts.
Fasten off.
Sew the nose and embroider the mouth onto the snout.

Sew the snout, eyes and ears onto the hat.
For sizes A and B sew two stripes on each side and two at the top of the head.
For size C sew three stripes on each side and two at the top of the head.
Weave in loose ends.

TIGER BOOTIES

YARN

 25g DK Orange

● 25g DK Black

Scrap yarn DK White
Scrap yarn DK Yellow (optional)

SIZES

A: Newborn – 3 months
B: 3 months – 6 months
C: 6 months – 1 year

TOOLS

3.5mm hook
Tapestry needle

TENSION

9 sts x 4 rows = 6cm/2¾in
measured over treble crochet

PATTERN NOTES

If you want to make bear
booties instead use the basic
bootie pattern from the giraffe
in brown yarn then use this
pattern to make the face.

BOOTIES

With orange
Rnd 1: 13 (15, 17)ch, 1tr in 4th ch
from hook, 1tr in each of next 8
(10, 12)ch, 6tr in last ch, working
back along the other side of chain
work 8 (10, 12)tr, 4tr in same st as
first tr of rnd, join - 28 (32, 36) sts.
Rnd 2: 3ch (counts as first tr), 10
(12, 14)tr, 2tr in each of next 4 sts,
10 (12, 14)tr, 2tr in each of next 3
sts, 1tr in same st as starting 3 ch,
join - 36 (40, 44) sts.
Rnd 3: 2ch (counts as first htr),
1htr blo in each st around, join.
With black
Rnd 4: 2ch, 7 (9, 11)htr, [htr2tog,
1htr] 6 times, 10 (12, 14) htr, join -
30 (34, 38) sts.
With orange
Rnd 5: 2ch, 7 (9, 11)htr, [htr2tog,
1htr] 4 times, 10 (12, 14)htr, join -
26 (30, 34) sts.
With black
Rnd 6: 2ch, 5 (7, 9)htr, [htr2tog] 6
times, 8 (10, 12)htr, join - 20 (24,
28) sts.
With orange
Rnd 7: 2ch, 7 (9, 11)htr, [htr2tog]
twice, 8 (10, 12)htr, join - 18 (22,
26) sts.
With black
Rnd 8: 1ch, 3 (5, 7)dc, [dc2tog] 3
times, 1dc in each st to end, join -
15 (19, 23) sts.
With orange

SIZE A AND B ONLY

With orange

Rnd 9: 2ch, 1htr in each st to end, join.

With black

Rnd 10: 1ch, 1dc in each st to end, join.

With orange

Rnd 11: Rep Rnd 9.

Fasten off. Weave in ends.

SIZE C ONLY

With orange

Rnd 9: 2ch, 7htr, [htr2tog] twice, 1htr to end, join.

With black

Rnd 10: 2ch, 6htr, [htr2tog] twice, 1htr to end, join.

With orange

Rnd 11: 2ch, 1htr in each st to end, join.

With black

Rnd 12: 2ch, 1htr in each st to end, join.

Fasten off. Weave in ends.

FACE

With orange

Rnd 1: Magic ring, 3ch, 11tr in ring, join - 12 sts.

Rnd 2: 3ch, 2tr in each st around, 1tr in same st as 3ch, join - 24 sts.

Rnd 3: 4ch, 1htr in 3rd ch from hook, 1tr in last ch, miss 2 sts of Rnd 2, sl st in each of next 3 sts, 4ch, 1htr in 3rd ch from hook, 1tr in last ch, miss 2 sts of Rnd 2, sl st in next st.

Fasten off. Leave enough yarn for sewing.

SNOUT

With white

Rnd 1: Magic ring, 3ch, 9tr in ring, join - 10 sts.

Fasten off. Leave enough yarn for sewing.

EYES

With yellow (or white)

Rnd 1: Magic ring, 6dc in ring, join - 6 sts.

Fasten off. Leave enough yarn for sewing.

Sew the eyes and snout onto the face. Use black yarn to embroider on little dots for pupils, a small nose and smile, and a few stripes. Sew the face onto the front of the booties.

UNICORN BEANIE

Unicorns are one of the best-loved mythical creatures and legends date back to ancient times. Nowadays there are plenty of books, cartoons and clothes adorned with these beautiful beasts so this beanie will make a great accompaniment.

YARN

Size A (B, C)

 25g (25g, 50g) DK Lilac

25g DK Light Blue

10g DK Dark Purple

25g DK White

Scrap yarn DK Black

OTHER MATERIALS

A small amount of toy stuffing
(see notes)

SIZES

A: Preemie
B: Newborn – 3months
C: 6 months – 1 year and beyond

TOOLS

4mm hook
3mm hook (or 3.5mm)
Tapestry needle

TENSION

10 sts x 8 rows = 10cm/4in
measured over treble crochet

PATTERN NOTES

- The horn doesn't need to be
  stuffed, but you may want give
  it a stronger structure.
  See page 8.

- Only the horn is made with the
  3mm hook, so unless otherwise
  stated use the 4mm hook.

- 3ch at the beginning of a row
  counts as 1tr, 2ch counts as 1htr.

- The snout and curls are worked
  in rows not rounds so do not join
  and turn at the end of a row as
  usual.

- This pattern uses a double treble
  crochet (dtr); if you have not used
  this before it may be worth testing
  out a few times before starting.

BEANIE

With lilac

5ch. Join with a sl st in first ch to
form a ring.
Rnd 1: 3ch (counts as first tr here
and throughout), 9 (11, 11)tr in
ring, join - 10 (12, 12) sts.
Rnd 2: 3ch, [2tr in next st] 9 [11, 11]
times, 1tr in same st as starting 3
ch, join - 20 (24, 24) sts.
Rnd 3: 3ch, [2tr in next st, 1tr] 9
[11, 11] times, 2tr in next st, join -
30 (36, 36) sts.
Rnd 4: 3ch, [2tr in next st, 2tr] 9
[11, 11] times, 2tr in next st, 1tr, join
- 40 (48, 48) sts.

SIZE A & B ONLY

Rnds 5- 8: 3ch, 1tr in each st to
end, join.
*Size A only fasten off, weave in
end.*

SIZE B ONLY

Rnds 9-10: 3ch, 1tr in each st to
end, join.
*If making the hat for a baby
over 2 months, crochet an 11th
round of trebles.
Fasten off, weave in end.*

SIZE C ONLY

Rnd 5: 3ch, [2tr in next st, 3tr] 11
times, 2tr in next st, 2tr, join - 60
sts.
Rnds 6-14: 3ch, 1tr in each st to
end, join.
Fasten off, weave in end.

EARS

(make 2)
With lilac

SIZE A ONLY

Rnd 1: 3ch, 5htr in first ch, join - 6 sts.

Rnd 2: 2ch, 2htr in each of next 5 sts, 1htr in same st as 2ch, join - 12 sts.

Rnd 3: 2ch, [2htr in next st, 1htr] 5 times, 2htr in next st, join - 18 sts.

Rnds 4-5: 2ch, 1htr in each st to end, join.

Fasten off.

SIZE B ONLY

Rnd 1: 4ch, 5tr in first ch, join - 6 sts.

Rnd 2: 3ch, 2tr in each of next 5 sts, 1tr in next st as 3ch, join - 12 sts.

Rnd 3: 3ch, [2tr in next st, 1tr] 5 times, 2tr in next st, join - 18 sts.

Rnds 4-5: 3ch, 1tr in each st to end, join.

Fasten off.

SIZE C ONLY

Rnd 1: 4ch, 5tr in first ch, join - 6 sts.

Rnd 2: 3ch, 2tr in each of next 5 sts, 1tr in same st st as 3ch, join - 12 sts.

Rnd 3: 3ch, [2tr in next st, 1tr] 5 times, 2tr in next st, join - 18 sts.

Rnd 4: 3ch, [2tr in next st, 2tr] 5 times, 2tr in next st, 1tr, join - 24 sts.

Rnds 5-6: 3ch, 1tr in each st to end, join.

Fasten off.

HORN

3mm hook
With white

SIZE A ONLY

Rnd 1: Magic ring, 2ch, 5htr, join -
6 sts.
Rnd 2: 2ch, 2htr in each of next
5 sts, 1htr in same st as 2ch, join -
12 sts.
Rnds 3-6: 2ch, 1htr in each st to
end, join.

SIZE B AND C ONLY

Rnd 1: Magic ring, 3ch, 5tr in ring,
join - 6 sts.
Rnd 2: 3ch, 2tr in each of next 5 sts,
1tr in same st as 3ch, join - 12 sts.
Rnds 3-7: 3ch, 1tr in each st to
end, join.

EYES

(make 2)
With white
Rnd 1: Magic ring, 3ch, in ring work
5 (9, 11)tr and 3 (3, 4)dtr, join - 9 (13,
16) sts.
Fasten off.

PUPILS

(make 2)
With black

SIZE A ONLY

Rnd 1: 2ch, 3dc in first ch, join -
4 sts.
*Fasten off. Sew pupil onto the oval
white eye.*

SIZE B AND C ONLY

Rnd 1: 3ch, 3 (5)htr in first ch, join
- 4 (6) sts.
Fasten off.

CURLS

Make 6 (8, 8).
With blue
Row 1: 18 (23, 33)ch, 2tr in 4th ch
from hook, 3tr in each ch across -
45 (60, 90) sts.
Fasten off.

SNOUT

With dark purple

SIZE A ONLY

Row 1: Magic ring, 3ch, 5tr in ring.
Turn - 6 sts.
Row 2: 3ch, 1tr in same st as 3 ch,
2tr in each st to end - 12 sts.
Fasten off.

SIZE B ONLY

Row 1: Magic ring, 2ch, 5htr in
ring. Turn - 6 sts.
Row 2: 2ch, 1tr in same st as 2 ch,
2htr in each st to end. Turn -
12 sts.
Row 3: 2ch, 2htr in each of next
10 sts, 1htr in last st - 22 sts.
Fasten off.

SIZE C ONLY

Row 1: Magic ring 3ch, 5tr in ring.
Turn - 6 sts.
Row 2: 3ch, 1tr in same st as 3 ch,
2tr in each st across. Turn - 12 sts.
Row 3: 3ch, 2tr in each of next 10
sts, 1tr in last st - 22 sts.
Fasten off.

UNICORN BOOTIES

YARN

● 25g DK Lilac
Scrap yarn DK White
Scrap yarn DK Black
Scrap yarn DK Blue

OTHER MATERIALS

Toy stuffing (optional –
see pattern notes)

BOOTIES

With lilac
Rnd 1: 13 (15, 17)ch, 1tr in 4th ch
from hook, 1tr in each of next 8
(10, 12)ch, 6tr in last ch, working
back along the other side of chain
work 8 (10, 12)tr, 4tr in same st as
first tr of rnd, join - 28 (32, 36) sts.
Rnd 2: 3ch (counts as first tr), 10
(12, 14)tr, 2tr in each of next 4 sts,
10 (12, 14)tr, 2tr in each of next 3
sts, 1tr in same st as starting 3 ch,
join - 36 (40, 44) sts.
Rnd 3: 2ch (counts as first htr),
1htr blo in each st around, join.
Rnd 4: 2ch, 7 (9, 11)htr, [htr2tog,
1htr] 6 times, 10 (12, 14) htr, join -
30 (34, 38) sts.
Rnd 5: 2ch, 7 (9, 11)htr, [htr2tog,
1htr] 4 times, 10 (12, 14)htr, join -
26 (30, 34) sts.
Rnd 6: 2ch, 5 (7, 9)htr, [htr2tog] 6

SIZES

A: Newborn – 3 months
B: 3 months – 6 months
C: 6 months – 1 year

TOOLS

3.5mm hook
3mm hook
Tapestry needle
Stitch marker optional (or just use
a contrasting piece of yarn)

TENSION

9 sts x 4 rows = 6cm/2¾in
measured over treble crochet

PATTERN NOTES

- The head and horn are worked
  in continuous spirals using the
  amigurumi technique, without
  joining at the end of each
  round. Here you just begin
  the next round on top of the
  previous round. Use a stitch
  marker or contrasting piece of
  yarn to mark the first stitch in
  each round.

- Crochet the ears and horn of
  the unicorn before the head.

- The head can be stuffed with
  toy stuffing. See page 8.

times, 8 (10, 12)htr, join - 20 (24,
28) sts.
Rnd 7: 2ch, 7 (9, 11)htr, [htr2tog]
twice, 8 (10, 12)htr, join - 18 (22,
26) sts.

SIZE A AND B ONLY

Rnd 8-9: 2ch, 1htr in each st to
end, join.
Fasten off.

SIZE C ONLY

Rnd 8: 2ch, 9htr, [htr2tog] 4 times,
1htr in each st to end, join - 22 sts.
Rnd 9-10: 2ch, 1htr in each st to
end, join.
Fasten off.

HORN

With white
3mm hook
This is worked in a spiral, so instead of joining at the end of the round, just start on the top of the next round.
Rnd 1: Magic ring, 4dc in ring - 4 sts.
Rnds 2 - 4 (4, 6): 1dc in each st around.
Fasten off.

EARS

(make 2)
With lilac
3mm hook
Rnd 1: 4 (4, 5)ch, 1dc in second ch from hook, 1htr, 1 (1, 2)tr, join - 3 (3, 4) sts.
Fasten off.

HEAD

With lilac
Use a stitch marker at the start of every round.
Rnd 1: Magic ring, 6dc - 6 sts.
Rnd 2: 2dc in each st around - 12 sts.
Rnds 3-5: 1dc in each st around.
Rnd 6: [2dc in next st, 1dc] 6 times - 18 sts.
Rnds 7-10: 1dc in each st around.

SIZE A AND B ONLY

With black yarn embroider on little eyes.
Sew on the horn and ears.
Rnd 11: [Dc2tog] 9 times - 9 sts.
Begin to stuff.
Rnd 12: Dc2tog around until the gap closes.
Fasten off.

SIZE C ONLY

Rnds 11-12: 1dc in each st around.
With black yarn embroider on little eyes.
Sew on the horn and ears.
Rnd 13: [Dc2tog] 9 times - 9 sts.
Begin to stuff.
Rnd 14: Dc2tog around until the gap closes.
Fasten off.

Tie scrap pieces of blue yarn to create the mane.
Sew the head to the bootie.
Optional – use scrap yarn to create a tail.

RAINBOW BEANIE HAT

Somewhere over the rainbow is this bright hat to bring sunshine to a rainy day.

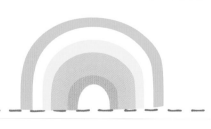

YARN

- 25g DK Light Blue
- 25g DK Light Green
- 10g DK Red
- 10g DK Orange
- 10g DK Yellow
- 10g DK Purple

SIZES

A: Newborn – 3 months
B: 3 months – 6 months
C: 6 months – 1 year

TOOLS

4mm hook
Tapestry needle

TENSION

10 sts x 8 rows = 10cm/4in
measured over treble crochet

PATTERN NOTES

- You could use small buttons in the middle of the flowers.

- When creating the rainbow, instead of turning at the end of each row, fasten off the yarn and begin every row at the same side.

BEANIE

With light blue
5ch. Join with a sl st in first ch to form a ring.
Rnd 1: 3ch (counts as first tr here and throughout), 9 (11, 11)tr in ring, join - 10 (12, 12) sts.
Rnd 2: 3ch, [2tr in next st] 9 [11, 11] times, 1tr in same st as starting 3 ch, join - 20 (24, 24) sts.
Rnd 3: 3ch, [2tr in next st, 1tr] 9 [11, 11] times, 2tr in next st, join - 30 (36, 36) sts.
Rnd 4: 3ch, [2tr in next st, 2tr] 9 [11, 11] times, 2tr in next st, 1tr, join - 40 (48, 48) sts.

SIZE A ONLY

Rnds 5-6: 3ch, 1tr in each st around, join - 40 sts.
Fasten off.
With green
Rnds 7-8: 3ch, 1tr in each st around, join.
Fasten off, weave in end.

SIZE B ONLY

Rnds 5-7: 3ch, 1tr in each st around, join - 48 sts.
With green
Rnds 8-10: 3ch, 1tr in each st around, join.
If making the hat for a baby over 2 months, crochet an 11th round of trebles.
Fasten off, weave in end.

SIZE C ONLY

Rnd 5: 3ch, [2tr in next st, 3tr] 11 times, 2tr in next st, 2tr, join - 60 sts.
Rnds 6-14: 3ch, 1tr in each st around, join.
Fasten off, weave in end.

FLOWERS

Make as many flowers as you like in any of the colours (all sizes).
Rnd 1: Magic ring, 1ch, (1dc, 1htr, 1dc, sl st) 5 times in ring, join.
Fasten off. With a contrasting colour, sew a little circle in the middle.

SUN

With yellow
Rnd 1: Magic ring, 3ch, 9 (11, 13)tr in ring, join - 10 (12, 14) sts.
Fasten off. Leave enough yarn to sew sunbeams.

RAINBOW

Do not turn but start at same side for each row. Fasten off each yarn leaving a 10cm/4in tail for sewing.

SIZE A ONLY

1ch at start of row does not count as a st.
With purple
Row 1: 3ch, 5htr in first ch - 6 sts
Fasten off.
With blue
Row 2: 1ch, 1dc in same st as ch, 2dc in each st to end - 10 sts.
Fasten off.
With green
Row 3: 1ch, 2dc in same st as ch, 1dc in each st to last st, 2dc in last st - 12 sts.
Fasten off.
With yellow
Row 4: As Row 3 - 14 sts.
Fasten off.
With orange
Row 5: As Row 3 - 16 sts.
Fasten off.
With red
Row 6: As Row 3 - 18 sts
Fasten off leaving a 15cm/6in tail.

SIZE B ONLY

1ch at start of row does not count as a st.
With purple
Row 1: 3ch, 5htr in first ch - 6 sts

Fasten off.
With blue
Row 2: 1ch, 1dc in same st as ch,
2dc in each of next 4 sts - 10 sts.
Fasten off.
With green
Row 3: 1ch, 1dc in same st as ch,
[2dc in next st, 1dc] 4 times, 2dc in
last st - 15 sts.
Fasten off.
With yellow
Row 4: 1ch, 1dc in same st as ch,
[2dc in next st, 2dc] 4 times, 2dc in
next st, 1dc - 20 sts. Fasten off.
With orange
Row 5: 1ch, 1dc in same st as ch,
[2dc in next st, 3dc] 4 times, 2dc in
next st, 2dc - 25 sts.
Fasten off.

With red
Row 6: 1ch, 1dc in same st as ch,
[2dc in next st, 4dc] 4 times, 2dc
in next st, 3dc - 30 sts
Fasten off leaving a 15cm/6in tail.

SIZE C ONLY

2ch at the start of a row counts as
first htr
With purple
Row 1: 3ch, 5htr in first ch - 6 sts.
Fasten off.
With blue
Row 2: 2ch, 2htr in each of next 4
sts 1htr - 10 sts.
Fasten off.
With green
Row 3: 2ch, [2htr in next st, 1htr] 4
times, 2htr in last st - 15 sts.

Fasten off.
With yellow
Row 4: 2ch, [2htr in next st, 2htr]
4 times, 2htr in next st, 1htr - 20
sts.
Fasten off.
With orange
Row 5: 2ch, [2htr in next st, 3htr] 4
times, 2htr in next st, 2htr - 25 sts.
Fasten off.
With red
Row 6: 2ch, [2htr in next st, 4htr]
4 times, 2htr in next st, 3htr - 30
sts.
Fasten off leaving a 15cm/6in tail.

Sew the sun, flowers and rainbow
onto hat, using photo as a guide
or in your own design.

RAINBOW BOOTIES

YARN

- 25g DK Light Blue
- 25g DK Light Green

Scrap DK yarn in purple, yellow, orange, red.

SIZES

A: Newborn – 3 months
B: 3 months – 6 months
C: 6 months – 1 year

TOOLS

3.5mm hook
Tapestry needle

TENSION

9 sts x 4 rows = 6cm/2¾in measured over trebles

PATTERN NOTES

- If you have enough scrap yarn you may wish to use different shades of green and blue in the rainbow to that which you have used for the main shoe.

- When crocheting the rainbows, start on the same side each time. So instead of turning your work at the end of the row, fasten off and begin the next row on the right again.

- In the rainbow, 1ch does not count as a stitch.

- You could embroider tiny dots on the grass area to look like flowers. This would be easiest to do after round 4 rather than when the whole bootie is complete.

BOOTIES

With green
Rnd 1: 13 (15, 17)ch, 1tr in 4th ch from hook, 1tr in each of next 8 (10, 12)ch, 6tr in last ch, working back along the other side of chain work 8 (10, 12)tr, 4tr in same st as first tr of rnd, join - 28 (32, 36) sts.
Rnd 2: 3ch (counts as first tr), 10 (12, 14)tr, 2tr in each of next 4 sts, 10 (12, 14)tr, 2tr in each of next 3 sts, 1tr in same st as starting 3 ch, join - 36 (40, 44) sts.
Rnd 3: 2ch (counts as first htr), 1htr blo in each st around, join.
Sizes A and B fasten off green and change to blue yarn. For size C continue with green.
Rnd 4: 2ch, 7 (9, 11)htr, [htr2tog, 1htr] 6 times, 10 (12, 14) htr, join - 30 (34, 38) sts.

Size C only: fasten off green, change to blue yarn.
Rnd 5: 2ch, 7 (9, 11)htr, [htr2tog, 1htr] 4 times, 10 (12, 14)htr, join - 26 (30, 34) sts.

Rnd 6: 2ch, 5 (7, 9)htr, [htr2tog] 6 times, 8 (10, 12)htr, join - 20 (24, 28) sts.
Rnd 7: 2ch, 7 (9, 11)htr, [htr2tog] twice, 8 (10, 12)htr, join - 18 (22, 26) sts.

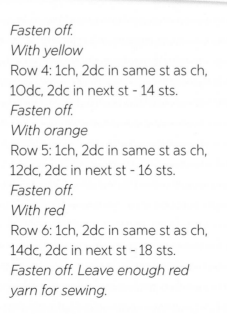

SIZE A AND B ONLY

Rnds 8-9: 2ch, 1htr in each st around, join - 18 (22) sts.
Fasten off. Weave in ends.

SIZE C ONLY

Rnd 8: 2ch, 9htr, [htr2tog] 4 times, 8htr, join - 22 sts.
Rnds 9-10: 2ch, 1htr in each st around, join.
Fasten off. Weave in ends.

RAINBOW

Do not turn but start at same side for each row. Fasten off each yarn leaving a 10cm/4in tail for sewing.

With purple
Row 1: 3ch, 5htr in first ch - 6 sts.
Fasten off. Leave a 10cm/4in yarn for sewing later.
With blue
Row 2: 1ch, 1dc in same st as ch, 2dc in each of next 4 sts, 1dc - 10 sts.
Fasten off.
With green
Row 3: 1ch, 2dc in same st as ch, 8dc, 2dc in next st - 12 sts.

Fasten off.
With yellow
Row 4: 1ch, 2dc in same st as ch, 10dc, 2dc in next st - 14 sts.
Fasten off.
With orange
Row 5: 1ch, 2dc in same st as ch, 12dc, 2dc in next st - 16 sts.
Fasten off.
With red
Row 6: 1ch, 2dc in same st as ch, 14dc, 2dc in next st - 18 sts.
Fasten off. Leave enough red yarn for sewing.

RIGHT SHOE

Sew the rainbow onto the right hand side using the red and purple yarn along the red and purple rows. Weave in all ends.

LEFT SHOE

Sew the rainbow onto the left hand side using the red and purple yarn along the red and purple rows. Weave in all ends.

SOCCER HAT

Babies have had their kicking practice while in the womb so they are ready to play when they are here.

YARN

● 25g DK Black

○ 25g DK White

SIZES

A: Newborn – 3 months
B: 6 months – 1 year and beyond

TOOLS

4mm hook
Tapestry needle

TENSION

10 sts x 8 rows = 10cm/4in
measured over treble crochet

PATTERN NOTES

This pattern uses hexagons, pentagons and semi-hexagons to create the ball shape. It's recommended that you block these before sewing together.

HEXAGONS

(make 5)
With white

SIZE A ONLY

Rnd 1: Magic ring, 3ch (counts as 1htr, 1ch), [1htr, 1ch] 5 times in ring, join to form a small hexagon - 12 sts.

Rnd 2: 2ch (counts as 1htr), *(1htr, 2ch, 1htr) in next 1ch-sp, 1htr in next st; rpt from * 4 more times, (1htr, 2ch, 1htr) in last 1ch-sp, join - 30 sts.
Fasten off.

SIZE B ONLY

Rnd 1: Magic ring, 4ch (counts as 1tr, 1ch), [1tr, 1ch] 5 times in ring, join to form a small hexagon - 12 sts.

Rnd 2: 3ch (counts as 1tr), *(1tr, 2ch, 1tr) in next 1ch-sp, 1tr in next st; rpt from * 4 more times, (1tr, 2ch, 1tr) in last 1ch-sp, join - 30 sts.
Fasten off.

SIZE B ONLY

Row 1: 5ch (first 4ch counts as 1tr, 1ch), (1tr, 1ch, 1tr) in first ch. Turn - 5 sts.
Row 2: 3ch (counts as 1tr), 1tr in same st as 3 ch, (1tr, 2ch, 2tr) in next ch-sp, 1tr in next st, (1tr, 2ch, 1tr) in next ch-sp, 2tr in last st - 12 sts.
Fasten off.

Sew five of the hexagons to each side of one of the pentagons. Sew the remaining pentagons in between the hexagons. Sew the half hexagons in between the pentagons.

BORDER

With white

Rnd 1: Start with 1ch (counts as first dc), continue in dc all the way around, creating 5 (6)dc in each pentagon and 5 (6)dc in each semi hexagon, join - 50 (60) sts.
With black
Rnds 2-3: 3ch, 1tr in each st around, join.
For size A, if the baby is over 2 months, crochet another round.
Rnd 4: 3ch, 1tr in each st around, join.
Fasten off. Weave in ends.

PENTAGONS

(make 6)
With black

SIZE A ONLY

Rnd 1: Magic ring, 3ch (counts as 1htr, 1ch), [1htr, 1ch] 4 times in ring, join to form a small pentagon - 10 sts.
Rnd 2: 2ch (counts as 1htr), *(1htr, 2ch, 1htr) in next 1ch-sp, 1htr in next st; rpt from * 3 more times, (1htr, 2ch, 1htr) in last 1ch-sp, join - 25 sts.
Fasten off.

SIZE B ONLY

Rnd 1: Magic ring, 4ch (counts as 1tr, 1ch), [1tr, 1ch] 4 times in ring, join to form a small pentagon - 10 sts.

Rnd 2: 3ch (counts as 1tr), *(1tr, 2ch, 1tr) in next 1ch-sp, 1tr in next st; rpt from * 3 more times, (1tr, 2ch, 1tr) in last 1ch-sp, join - 25 sts.
Fasten off.

SEMI-HEXAGONS

(make 5)
With white

SIZE A ONLY

Row 1: 4ch (first 3ch counts as 1htr, 1ch), (1htr, 1ch, 1htr) in first ch. Turn - 5 sts.
Row 2: 2ch (counts as 1htr), 1htr in same st as 2 ch, (1htr, 2ch, 2htr) in next ch-sp, 1htr in next st, (1htr, 2ch, 1htr) in next ch-sp, 2htr in last st - 12 sts.
Fasten off.

SOCCER BOOTS

YARN

 25g DK Black

○ 25g DK White

SIZES

A: Newborn – 3 months
B: 3 months – 6 months
C: 6 months – 1 year

TOOLS

3.5mm hook
Tapestry needle

TENSION

9 sts x 4 rows = 6cm/2¾in
measured over treble crochet

PATTERN NOTES

- Not interested in soccer?
  Omit the studs and use the
  pattern to create sneakers in
  a different colour.

- When it comes to the laces,
  please exercise caution
  around babies and choking
  hazards.

BOOTS

With white
Rnd 1: 13 (15, 17)ch, 1tr in 4th ch
from hook, 1tr in each of next 8
(10, 12)ch, 6tr in last ch, working
back along the other side of chain
work 8 (10, 12)tr, 4tr in same st as
first tr of rnd, join - 28 (32, 36) sts.
Rnd 2: 3ch, 10 (12, 14)tr, 2tr in
each of next 4 sts, 10 (12, 14)tr, 2tr
in each of next 3 sts, 1tr in same
st as starting 3 ch, join - 36 (40,
44) sts.
Rnd 3: 1ch, 1dc blo in same st as
1ch, 10 (12, 14)dc blo, 2tr blo in
each of next 8 sts, 1dc blo in each
st to end, join - 44 (48, 52) sts.
Fasten off.
With black
Rnd 4: 2ch, 7 (9, 11)htr, [htr2tog,

1htr] 6 times, 1htr to end, join - 30
(34, 38) sts.
Rnd 5: 2ch, 7 (9, 11)htr, [htr2tog,
1htr] 4 times, 1htr to end, join - 26
(30, 34) sts.
Rnd 6: 2ch, 5 (7, 9)htr, [htr2tog] 6
times, 1htr to end, join - 20 (24,
28) sts.
Fasten off.
Row 7: Miss 12 (14, 16) sts, rejoin
yarn after sixth htr2tog of Rnd 6,
1ch, 13 (17, 23)dc. Turn - 14 (18, 24)
sts.
Rows 8-11: 1ch, 13 (17, 23)dc. Turn
- 14 (18, 24) sts.
Fasten off size A and B.

SIZE C ONLY

Row 12: 1ch, 23dc. Turn - 24dc.
Fasten off.

TONGUE

With black

You should have 4 sts in the gap you have created. Start one st before this. 1ch at the beginning of a row counts as 1 st.

Rows 1-2: 1ch, 5dc. Turn - 6dc.

Row 3: 1ch, 1dc, 2dc in each of next 2 sts, 1dc in each of next 2 sts. Turn - 8 sts.

Rows 4-6: 1ch, 7dc. Turn.

For size A, fasten off.

Row 7: 1ch, 7dc. Turn.

For size B, fasten off.

SIZE C ONLY

Row 8: 1ch, 7dc. Turn.

Fasten off.

STUDS

With white

Size A make 6; sizes B and C make 8

Rnd 1: Magic ring. 6dc in ring, join - 6 sts.

Rnd 2: 1ch, 1dc in each st around, join.

Fasten off. Leave enough yarn for sewing on. Sew them onto the sole.

SHOELACES

With white

80ch.

Fasten off and weave in ends. Lace up at the front.

STRAWBERRY BEANIE HAT

Strawberries and Summer go hand in hand, so even in the coldest of months you'll be thinking of sunnier days. The baby is guaranteed to look berry cute!

YARN

Size A (B, C)

● 25g (25g, 50g) DK Red

● 10g DK Green

○ 5g DK Yellow

SIZES

A: Preemie
B: Newborn – 3 months
C: 6 months – 1 year and beyond

TOOLS

4mm hook
Tapestry needle

TENSION

10 sts x 8 rows = 10cm/4in
measured over treble crochet

PATTERN NOTES

Instead of stitching on yellow yarn
for the seeds you could use little
beads or buttons.

BEANIE

With green
All sizes
Rnd 1: 4ch, 9 (11, 11)tr in first ch,
join - 10 (12, 12) sts.
Rnd 2: 3ch, 1tr blo in each st to
end, join.

Rnd 3: 3ch, 1tr in each st to end,
join.
Rnd 4: 3ch, [2tr in next st] 9 [11,
11] times, 1tr in same st as starting
3 ch, join - 20 (24, 24) sts.
Fasten off.

With red
Rnd 5: 3ch, [2tr in next st, 1tr] 9
[11, 11] times, 2tr in next st, join -
30 [36, 36] sts.
Rnd 6: 3ch, [2tr in next st, 2tr] 9
[11, 11] times, 2tr in next st, 1tr, join
- 40 [48, 48] sts.

SIZE A ONLY

Rnds 7-10: 3ch, 1tr in each st to end, join.
Fasten off. Weave in ends.

SIZE B ONLY

Rnds 7-12: 3ch, 1tr in each st to end, join.
For babies that are over 2 months, crochet a 13th round in trebles.
Fasten off. Weave in ends.

SIZE C ONLY

Rnd 7: 3ch, [2tr in next st, 3tr] 11 times, 2tr in next st, 2tr, join - 60 sts.
Rnds 8-14: 3ch, 1tr in each st to end, join.

LEAVES

(make 8)
With green

SIZE A ONLY

Row 1: 7ch, starting in 2nd ch from hook, sl st, 1dc, 1htr, 3tr - 6 sts.
Fasten off.

SIZE B AND C ONLY

Row 1: 9ch, starting in 2nd ch from hook, sl st, 1dc, 1htr, 2tr, 3dtr - 8 sts.
Fasten off.

Sew the leaves onto the hat. Use the yellow yarn to stitch small seeds onto the hat. Weave in ends.

STRAWBERRY BOOTIES

YARN

- 25g DK Red
- 5g DK Green
- 5g DK Yellow

SIZES

A: Newborn – 3 months
B: 3 months – 6 months
C: 6 months – 1 year

TOOLS

3.5mm hook
Tapestry needle

TENSION

9 sts x 4 rows = 6cm/2¼in measured over treble crochet

PATTERN NOTES

- Cut yellow yarn into two 100cm strands.

- Sew the yellow seeds as you go along rather than at the end, don't fasten off until the end.

BOOTIES

(make 2)
All sizes
With red
Rnd 1: 13 (15, 17)ch, 1tr in 4th ch from hook, 1tr in each of next 8 (10, 12)ch, 6tr in last ch, working back along the other side of chain work 8 (10, 12)tr, 4tr in same st as first tr of rnd, join - 28 (32, 36) sts.
Rnd 2: 3ch (counts as first tr), 10 (12, 14)tr, 2tr in each of next 4 sts, 10 (12, 14)tr, 2tr in each of next 3 sts, 1tr in same st as starting 3 ch, join - 36 (40, 44) sts.
Rnd 3: 2ch (counts as first htr), 1htr blo in each st around, join.
Rnd 4: 2ch, 7 (9, 11)htr, [htr2tog, 1htr] 6 times, 10 (12, 14) htr, join - 30 (34, 38) sts.
Rnd 5: 2ch, 7 (9, 11)htr, [htr2tog, 1htr] 4 times, 10 (12, 14)htr, join - 26 (30, 34) sts.
Rnd 6: 2ch, 5 (7, 9)htr, [htr2tog] 6 times, 8 (10, 12)htr, join - 20 (24, 28) sts.
Use yellow yarn to embroider small seeds at regular intervals.
Rnd 7: 2ch, 7 (9, 11)htr, [htr2tog] twice, 8 (10, 12)htr, join - 18 (22, 26) sts.

SIZE A AND B ONLY

Rnds 8 -9: 1ch, 1dc in each st to end, join.
Fasten off.
Use yellow yarn again to sew seeds around the bootie.
With green
Rnd 10: 1ch, 1dc, 1tr in st two rows below, [2dc, 1tr in st two rows below] to last st, 1dc, join.
Fasten off, weave in ends.

SIZE C ONLY

Rnd 8: 2ch, 9htr, [htr2tog] 4 times, 1htr in each st to end, join - 22 sts.
Rnd 9: 2ch, 1htr in each st to end, join.
Rnds 10-11: 1ch, 1dc in each st to end, join.
Fasten off red.

Use yellow yarn again to sew seeds around the bootie.
With green
Rnd 12: 1ch, 1dc, 1tr in st two rows below, [2dc, 1tr in st two rows below] to last 2 sts, 2dc, join.
Fasten off, weave in ends.

CUPCAKE HAT

When your baby is as scrummy as a cupcake this is the perfect hat to adorn its sweet little head! The colourful sprinkles can be made with any bits of scrap yarn you have to hand.

YARN

Size A (B, C)

 25g (25g, 50g) DK Blue

● 25g DK Light Brown

● 10g DK Red

Scrap yarn in whichever colours you want

OTHER MATERIALS

A small amount of toy stuffing (optional, see pattern notes)

SIZES

A: Preemie
B: Newborn – 3 months
C: 6 months – 1 year and beyond

TOOLS

4mm hook
3.5mm hook
Tapestry needle
Stitch marker (optional – use a contrasting piece of yarn)

TENSION

10 sts x 8 rows = 10cm/4in measured over treble crochet

PATTERN NOTES

- The cherry uses the amigurumi technique working in continuous spirals rather than joining at the end of each round. Here you just begin the next round on top of the previous round. Use a stitch marker or contrasting piece of yarn to mark the first stitch in each round.

- The cherry can be stuffed with toy stuffing. See page 8.

- This pattern uses front post trebles (fptr) technique and double trebles (dtr); if you're not familiar with these it may be worth practising before starting the hat.

BEANIE

With blue and 4mm hook
5ch. Join with a sl st in first ch to form a ring.
Rnd 1: 3ch (counts as first tr here and throughout), 9 (11, 11)tr in ring, join - 10 (12, 12) sts.
Rnd 2: 3ch, [2tr blo in next st] 9 [11, 11] times, 1tr blo in same st as starting 3 ch, join - 20 (24, 24) sts.
Rnd 3: 3ch, [2tr blo in next st, 1tr blo] 9 [11, 11] times, 2tr blo in next st, join - 30 (36, 36) sts.
Rnd 4: 3ch, [2tr blo in next st, 2tr blo] 9 [11, 11] times, 2tr blo in next st, 1tr blo, join - 40 (48, 48) sts.

SIZE A AND B ONLY

Rnds 5 - 6: 3ch, 1tr blo in each st to end, join - 40 (48) sts.

Change to brown yarn, but do not fasten off blue, leave this at the front of your piece so you can use it later.

With brown
Rnd 7: 3ch, 1htr blo in each st to end, join.

NB: every alternate treble will be worked around the front post of the previous row's treble (written as fptr).
Rnds 8-9: 3ch, [1fptr, 1tr] to last st, 1fptr, join.
Fasten off for size A.

SIZE A ONLY

Go back to blue yarn to create the icing "frill" on top of Rnd 8 working in unused front loops of Rnd 7.

Frill: *(1sl st, 1htr) in next st, 2tr, (1htr, 1sl st) in next st; rpt from * to end, join - 40 sts.

Fasten off.

Embroider small stitches of scrap yarn to create sprinkles.

SIZE B ONLY

Rnds 10-11: Rpt Rnd 8.

If making the hat for a baby over 2 months, crochet a 12th round. Fasten off. Weave in end.

Go back to blue yarn to create the icing "frill" on top of Rnd 8 working in unused front loops of Rnd 7.

Frill: *(1sl st, 1htr) in next st, 1tr, 2dtr, 1tr, (1htr, 1sl st) in next st; rpt from * to end, join - 48 sts.

Embroider small stitches of scrap yarn to create sprinkles.

SIZE C ONLY

Rnd 5: 3ch, [2tr blo in next st, 3tr blo] 11 times, 2tr blo in next st, 2tr blo, join - 60 sts.

Rnds 6-9: 3ch, 1tr blo in each st around, join.

Change to light brown yarn, but do not fasten off blue, leave this at the front of your piece so you can use it later.

Rnd 10: 3ch, 1tr blo in each st around, join.

NB: every alternate treble will be worked around the front post of the previous row's treble (written as fptr).

Rnds 11-14: 3ch, [1fptr, 1tr] to last st, 1fptr, join.

Fasten off. Weave in end.

Go back to blue yarn to create the icing "frill" on top of Rnd 10 working in unused front loops of Rnd 9.

Frill: *(1sl st, 1htr) in next st, 1tr, 2dtr, 1tr, (1htr, 1sl st) in next st; rpt from * to end, join - 60 sts.

CHERRY

With red and 3.5mm hook
This is worked using the amigurumi technique using continuous spirals without joining at the end of each round. Here you just begin the next round on top of the previous round. Use a stitch marker or contrasting piece of yarn to mark the first stitch in each row.

SIZE A AND B ONLY

Magic ring
Rnd 1: 6dc in ring - 6 sts.
Rnd 2: 2dc in each st around - 12 sts.
Rnd 3: [2dc in next st, 1dc] 6 times - 18 sts.
Rnds 4-6: 1dc in each st around.
Rnd 7: [Dc2tog, 1dc] 6 times - 12 sts.
Insert stuffing into the cherry.
Rnd 8: Dc2tog around until the gap closes
Fasten off. Leave enough yarn to sew this onto the top of the hat.

SIZE C ONLY

Magic ring
Rnd 1: 6dc in ring - 6 sts.
Rnd 2: 2dc in each st around - 12 sts.
Rnd 3: [2dc in next st, 1dc] 6 times - 18 sts
Rnd 4: [2dc in next st, 2dc] 6 times - 24 sts.
Rnds 5-7: 1dc in each st around.

Rnd 8: [Dc2tog, 2dc] 6 times - 18 sts.
Rnd 9: [Dc2tog, 1dc] 6 times - 12 sts.
Insert stuffing into the cherry.
Rnd 10: Dc2tog around until the gap closes
Fasten off. Leave enough yarn to sew this onto the top of the hat.

CUPCAKE BOOTIES

YARN

● 25g DK Brown

● 25g DK Blue

Scrap yarn for sprinkles

SIZES

A: Newborn – 3 months
B: 3 months – 6 months
C: 6 months – 1 year

TOOLS

3.5mm hook
Tapestry needle

TENSION

9 sts x 4 rows = 6cm/2¼in
measured over treble crochet

PATTERN NOTES

This pattern uses the picot
stitch: 1dc, 3ch, insert hook into
front post of first dc, pull yarn
through so you now have two
loops on your hook, pull yarn
through both loops, 1dc into
next stitch.

BOOTIES

With brown
Rnd 1: 13 (15, 17)ch, 1tr in 4th ch
from hook, 1tr in each of next 8
(10, 12)ch, 6tr in last st, working
back along the other side of chain
work 8 (10, 12)tr, 4tr in same st as
first tr of rnd, join - 28 (32, 36) sts.
Rnd 2: 3ch (counts as first tr), 10
(12, 14)tr, 2tr in each of next 4 sts,
10 (12, 14)tr, 2tr in each of next 3
sts, 1tr in same st as starting 3 ch,
join - 36 (40, 44) sts.
Rnd 3: 2ch (counts as first htr),
1htr blo in each st around, join.
Rnd 4: 2ch, 7 (9, 11) htr, [htr2tog,
1htr] 6 times, 10 (12, 14) htr, join -
30 (34, 38) sts.
Rnd 5: 2ch, 7 (9, 11)htr, [htr2tog,
1htr] 4 times, 10 (12, 14)htr, join -
26 (30, 34) sts.

Rnd 6: 2ch, 5 (7, 9)htr, [htr2tog] 6
times, 8 (10, 12)htr, join - 20 (24,
28) sts.
Rnd 7: 2ch, 7 (9, 11)htr, [htr2tog]
twice, 8 (10, 12)htr, join - 18 (22, 26)
sts.

SIZE A & B ONLY

Fasten off.
With blue

Rnds 8-9: 2ch, 1htr in each st
around, join - 18 (22) sts.
*Turn your work around and begin
working from the inside of the
bootie.*
Rnd 10: 2ch, 1htr in each st around,
join.
Rnd 11: 1ch, 1dc in same st, *(1htr,
1tr, 1dtr) all in next st, (1dtr, 1tr, 1htr)
all in next st, picot (see pattern
notes); rpt from * to end, join.
Fasten off.

SIZE C ONLY

Rnd 8: 2ch, 9htr, [htr2tog] 4 times, 7htr, join - 22 sts.
Fasten off.
With blue
Rnds 9-10: 2ch, 1htr in each st around, join.
Turn your work around and begin working from the inside of the bootie.
Rnd 11: 2ch, 1htr in each st around, join.
Rnd 12: 1ch, 1dc in same st, *(1htr, 1tr, 1dtr) all in next st, (1dtr, 1tr, 1htr) all in next st, picot; rpt from * to end, join.
Fasten off.
Embroider scrap yarn or beads randomly on the blue to create sprinkles.
Weave in ends.

ROAD TRIP BEANIE

Perfect for when you're hitting the road on an adventure to a friend's house or a day out of fun!

YARN

- 25g DK Blue
- 10g DK Green
- 10g DK Grey
- 10g DK White
- 10g DK Yellow
- 25g DK Red (or any mix colour for the cars)

Scrap yarn DK Black

SIZES

A: Preemie
B: Newborn – 3 months
C: 6 months – 1 year and beyond

TOOLS

4mm hook
Tapestry needle

TENSION

10 sts x 8 rows = 10cm/4in measured over treble crochet

PATTERN NOTES

For the car appliqué, 1ch at the start of a row does not count as a dc.

BEANIE

With blue
5ch. Join with a sl st in first ch to form a ring.
Rnd 1: 3ch (counts as first tr here and throughout), 9 (11, 11)tr in ring, join - 10 (12, 12) sts.
Rnd 2: 3ch, [2tr in next st] 9 [11, 11] times, 1tr in same st as starting 3 ch, join - 20 (24, 24) sts.
Rnd 3: 3ch, [2tr in next st, 1tr] 9 [11, 11] times, 2tr in next st, join - 30 (36, 36) sts.
Rnd 4: 3ch, [2tr in next st, 2tr] 9 [11, 11] times, 2tr in next st, 1tr, join - 40 (48, 48) sts.

SIZE A ONLY

Rnds 5-6: 3ch, 1tr in each st to end, join - 40 sts.
Fasten off blue.
With green
Rnd 7: 1ch, 1dc in each st to end, join.
Fasten off.
With grey
Rnd 8: 2ch (counts as first st), 1htr in each st to end, join.

Rnd 9: 2ch, 1htr, [3htr using white, 2htr using grey] to last 3 sts, 3htr using white, join.
Fasten off white.
With grey
Rnd 10: 2ch, 1htr in each st to end, join.
Fasten off.
With green
Rnd 11: 1ch, 1dc in each st to end, join.
Fasten off. Weave in ends.

SIZE B ONLY

Rnds 5-6: 3ch, 1tr in each st to end, join - 48 sts.
Fasten off blue.

With green
Rnd 7: 1ch, 1dc in each st to end, join.
With grey
Rnd 8: 3ch, 1tr in each st to end, join.
Rnd 9: 3ch, 1tr, [5tr using white, 3tr using grey] 5 times, 5tr using white, 1tr using grey, join.
Fasten off white.
With grey
Rnd 10: 3ch, 1tr in each st to end, join.
Fasten off grey.
With green
Rnd 11: 1ch, 1dc in each st to end, join.
Fasten off. Weave in ends.

SIZE C ONLY

Rnd 5: 3ch, [2tr in next st, 3tr] 11 times, 2tr in same st, 2tr, join - 60 sts.

Rnds 6 -9: 3ch, 1tr in each st to end, join.

Fasten off.

With green

Rnd 10: 1ch, 1dc in each st to end, join.

Fasten off.

With grey

Rnd 11: 1ch, 1dc in each st to end, join.

Rnd 12: 2ch, 1htr, [6htr using white, 4htr using grey] 5 times, 6htr using white, 2htr using grey, join.

Fasten off white.

With grey

Rnd 13: 2ch, 1htr in each st to end, join.

Fasten off grey.

With green

Rnd 14: 1ch, 1dc in each st to end, join.

Fasten off.

Weave in ends.

SUN

With yellow

Rnd 1: Magic ring, 3ch, 11 (11, 13)tr in ring, join - 12 (12, 14) sts.

Fasten off. Sew onto hat. Sew lines to create sunbeams.

CAR

(make 1-4)

With red

SIZE A AND B

Row 1: 11ch, 1dc in 2nd ch from hook, and in each ch to end. Turn - 10 sts.

Rows 2-3: 1ch, 1dc in each st to end. Turn.

Row 4: 1ch, 6dc, sl st in next st. Turn - 6dc.

Row 5: Sl st, 1ch, 5dc, sl st. Turn - 5dc.

Row 6: Sl st, 1ch, 4dc, sl st. Turn - 4dc.

Fasten off, leave enough yarn for sewing.

SIZE C

Row 1: 15ch, 1dc in 2nd ch from hook, and in each ch to end. Turn - 14 sts.

Rows 2-4: 1ch, 1dc in each st to end. Turn.

Row 5: 1ch, 9dc, sl st in next st. turn - 9dc.

Row 6: Sl st, 1ch, 9dc. Turn.

Row 7: Sl st, 7dc, sl st. Turn - 7dc.

Row 8: Sl st, 6dc, sl st. Turn - 6dc.

Row 9: Sl st, 5dc, sl st. Turn - 5dc.

Fasten off.

With white yarn, embroider on window.

WHEELS

(make 2)

With black

Rnd 1: Magic ring, 2ch, 5htr in ring, join - 6 sts.

Fasten off.

Sew cars onto the hat adding two wheels per car. Embroider the window using scraps of white.

CAR BOOTIES

YARN

 25g DK Blue

● 10g DK Black

Scrap yarn DK White
Scrap yarn DK Yellow

SIZES

A: Newborn – 3 months
B: 3 months – 6 months
C: 6 months – 1 year

TOOLS

3.5mm hook
Tapestry needle

TENSION

9 sts x 4 rows = 6cm/2¼in
measured over treble crochet

PATTERN NOTES

The window is crocheted in
rows, so turn at the end of
every row.

BOOTIES

With blue

Rnd 1: 13 (15, 17)ch, 1tr in 4th ch
from hook, 1tr in each of next 8
(10, 12)ch, 6tr in last ch, working
back along the other side of chain
work 8 (10, 12)tr, 4tr in same st as
first tr of rnd, join - 28 (32, 36) sts.
Rnd 2: 3ch (counts as first tr), 10
(12, 14)tr, 2tr in each of next 4 sts,
10 (12, 14)tr, 2tr in each of next 3
sts, 1tr in same st as starting 3 ch,
join - 36 (40, 44) sts.
Rnd 3: 2ch (counts as first htr),
1htr blo in each st around, join.
Rnd 4: 2ch, 7 (9, 11)htr, [htr2tog,
1htr] 6 times, 10 (12, 14) htr, join -
30 (34, 38) sts.

Rnd 5: 2ch, 7 (9, 11)htr, [htr2tog,
1htr] 4 times, 10 (12, 14)htr, join -
26 (30, 34) sts.
Rnd 6: 2ch, 5 (7, 9)htr, [htr2tog] 6
times, 8 (10, 12)htr, join - 20 (24,
28) sts.

SIZE A AND B ONLY

Rnd 7: 1ch, 7 (9)dc, [htr2tog]
twice, 1dc to end, join - 18 (22) sts.
Fasten off. Weave in ends.

SIZE C ONLY

Rnd 7: 1ch, 9dc, [tr2tog] 4 times,
1dc to end, join - 24 sts.
Rnd 8: 1ch, 10dc, htr2tog, 1dc to
end, join - 23 sts.
Fasten off. Weave in ends.

WHEELS

(make 4)
With black
Rnd 1: Magic ring, 2ch, 7 (9, 9)htr, join - 8 (10, 10) sts.
Fasten off.
With the white yarn embroider three lines that meet in the middle to create a little star.
Sew two on each side.

HEADLIGHTS

(make 2)
With yellow
Rnd 1: Magic ring, 1ch, 4dc in ring, join - 4 sts.
Fasten off.
Sew onto the front.

WINDOW

With white
Row 1: 7 (9, 11)ch, 1dc in 2nd ch from hook and in each ch to end. Turn - 6 (8, 10) sts.
Rows 2-3: 1ch, 1dc to end. Turn.
For size A, fasten off.
Sew onto the front of the shoe.

SIZE B AND C

Row 4: 1ch, 1dc to end. Turn - 8 (10) sts.
For size B, fasten off.
Sew onto the front of the shoe.

SIZE C ONLY

Row 5: 1ch, 1dc to end.
Fasten off.
Sew onto the front of the shoe.

SANTA HAT

A baby's first Christmas is so special and this hat would look adorable for all those meet ups and occasions during the festive season.

YARN

Size A (B, C)

● 25g (50g, 50g) DK Red

○ 25g DK White

(see pattern notes)

NOTIONS

Fluffy white pom pom

SIZES

A: Preemie

B: Newborn – 3 months

C: 6 months – 1 year and beyond

TOOLS

4mm hook

Tapestry needle

TENSION

10 sts x 8 rows = 10cm/4in
measured over treble crochet

PATTERN NOTES

- For the trim, you could you use some fluffy white yarn in DK eg James C Brett Flutterby Quick Knit which will give the booties a snuggly texture. Check the hook size as recommended on the label.

- Work all three sizes the same to end of Rnd 23.

BEANIE

With red

Rnd 1: Magic ring, 3ch, 5tr in ring, join – 6 sts.

Rnds 2-3: 3ch, 1tr in each st around, join.

Rnd 4: 3ch, 1tr, 2tr in next st, 2tr, 2tr in next st, join - 8 sts.

Rnd 5: 3ch, 1tr in each st around, join.

Rnd 6: 3ch, 2tr, 2tr in next st, 3tr, 2tr in next st, join - 10 sts.

Rnd 7: 3ch, 1tr in each st around, join.

Rnd 8: 3ch, 3tr, 2tr in next st, 4tr, 2tr in next st, join - 12 sts.

Rnd 9: 3ch, 1tr in each st around, join.

Rnd 10: 3ch, 4tr, 2tr in same st, 5tr, 2tr in next st, join - 14 sts.

Rnd 11: 3ch, 1tr into each st to end, join.

Rnd 12: 3ch, 5tr, 2tr in next st, 6tr, 2tr in next st, join - 16 sts.

Rnd 13: 3ch, 1tr in each st around, join.

Rnd 14: 3ch, 2tr, 2tr in next st, [3tr, 2tr in next st] 3 times, join - 20 sts.

Rnd 15: 3ch, 1tr in each st around, join.

Rnd 16: 3ch, 2tr, 2tr in next st, [3tr, 2tr in next st] 4 times, join - 25 sts.

Rnd 17: 3ch, 1tr in each st around, join.

Rnd 18: 3ch, 3tr, 2tr in next st, [4tr, 2tr in next st] 4 times, join - 30 sts.

Rnd 19: 3ch, 1tr in each st around, join.

Rnd 20: 3ch, 3tr, 2tr in next st, [4tr, 2tr in next st] 5 times, join - 36 sts.

Rnd 21: 3ch, 1tr in each st around, join.

Rnd 22: 3ch, 4tr, 2tr in next st, [5tr, 2tr in next st] 5 times, join - 42 sts.

Rnd 23: 3ch, 1tr in each st around, join.

SIZE A ONLY

Rnds 24-25: 3ch, 1tr in each st around, join.

Fasten off.

With white

(change hook if necessary)

Rnds 26-27: 3ch, 1tr in each st around, join.

Fasten off. Weave in ends.

SIZE B ONLY

Rnd 24: 3ch, 5tr, 2tr in next st, [6tr, 2tr in next st] 5 times, join – 48 sts.

Rnd 25: 3ch, 1tr in each st around, join.

Fasten off.

With white yarn (change hook if necessary)

Rnds 26-27: 3ch, 1tr in each st around, join.

Fasten off. Weave in ends.

SIZE C ONLY

Rnd 24: 3ch, 5tr, 2tr in next st, [6tr, 2tr in next st] 5 times, join – 48 sts.

Rnd 25: 3ch, 1tr in each st around, join.

Rnd 26: 3ch, 6tr, 2tr in next st, [7tr, 2tr in next st] 5 times, join – 54 sts.

Rnd 27: 3ch, 1tr in each st around, join.

Rnd 28: 3ch, 7tr, 2tr in next st, [8tr, 2tr in next st] 5 times, join – 60 sts.

Rnd 29: 3ch, 4tr, 2tr in next st, [5tr, 2tr in next st] 9 times, join – 70 sts.

Fasten off.

With white

(change hook if necessary)

Rnds 30-31: 3ch, 1tr in each st around, join.

Fasten off.

Weave in ends.

Affix the pom pom to the end.

SNUGGLY SANTA BOOTIES

YARN

 25g DK Red

○ 25g DK White
(see pattern notes)

SIZES

A: Newborn – 3 months
B: 3 months – 6 months
C: 6 months – 1 year

TOOLS

3.5mm hook
4mm hook (optional)
Tapestry needle

TENSION

9 sts x 4 rows = 6cm/2¼in
measured over treble crochet

PATTERN NOTES

For the trim, you could you
use some fluffy white yarn eg
James C Brett Flutterby Quick
Knit which will give the booties
a snuggly texture. If you use
this type of yarn you may
need to switch to 4mm hook.
Check the recommended
hook size on the label.

BOOTIES

With red
Rnd 1: 13 (15, 17)ch, 1tr in 4th ch
from hook, 1tr in each of next 8
(10, 12)ch, 6tr in last ch, working
back along the other side of chain
work 8 (10, 12)tr, 4tr in same st as
first tr of rnd, join - 28 (32, 36) sts.
Rnd 2: 3ch (counts as first tr), 10
(12, 14)tr, 2tr in each of next 4 sts,
10 (12, 14)tr, 2tr in each of next 3
sts, 1tr in same st as starting 3 ch,
join - 36 (40, 44) sts.
Rnd 3: 2ch (counts as first htr),
1htr blo in each st around, join.
Rnd 4: 2ch, 7 (9, 11)htr, [htr2tog,
1htr] 6 times, 10 (12, 14) htr, join -
30 (34, 38) sts.
Rnd 5: 2ch, 7 (9, 11)htr, [htr2tog,
1htr] 4 times, 10 (12, 14)htr, join -
26 (30, 34) sts.

Rnd 6: 2ch, 5 (7, 9)htr, [htr2tog] 6
times, 8 (10, 12)htr, join - 20 (24,
28) sts.
Rnd 7: 2ch, 7 (9, 11)htr, [htr2tog]
twice, 8 (10, 12)htr, join - 18 (22,
26) sts.

SIZE A & B ONLY

*With white
(change hook if necessary)*
Rnds 8-9: 2ch, 1htr in each st to
end, join.
Fasten off.

SIZE C ONLY

*With white
(change hook if necessary)*
Rnd 8: 2ch, 9htr, [htr2tog] 4 times,
1htr in each st to end, join - 22 sts.
Rnds 9-10: 2ch, 1htr in each st
around, join.
Fasten off.

ACKNOWLEDGEMENTS

Thank you to Jayne Parsons and all at Bloomsbury Publishers and Herbert Press for taking a chance on my ideas and giving me this wonderful opportunity. Masses of appreciation to all the fantastic team who turned my ramblings and woolly goods into a serviceable book: Andy Chapman, David Macartney and Dominic Fagan at Plum5; Rachel Vowles and her technical editing skills; Agata Sroka and Patrycja Szlosarczyk at Tiny Toes by Aggi and the additional photography talents of Roxanne Bennett, Scarlett McQueen and Charlie West.

Thank you to the amazingly gorgeous models for showing off my cute creations, Emma, Luka, Eddie, Olivia and the twins Oliwier and Leon... and, of course, thank you to your lovely parents for their time and effort too.

Huge thanks to Kate Bodsworth for giving me a push start to make it all happen!

Special shout out goes to my cheerleaders in the Birdi family: Mum, Dad, Rani, Bobby, Shane, Kierthan, Rajan, Jayan, Sampuran and Tara. It's good to be in your team.

To the Hatchard and Hutchinson clan, Alan, Brenda, Laura, Faye, Matt and Lauren, thanks for all your support.

To my uni friends, who've been with me for years, and probably never guessed that one day I'd write a crochet book, but will never forgive me if they don't get a mention, Katie Wood, Helen O'Connell, Dan Brisk, Fred and Emma Vanderplank, Catherine Cashmore and Olivia Haseldine.

Thank you to Dr Nooreen Khan, for not having a clue about crafting but sending love and cupcakes, especially during lockdown and the ridiculous leg injury I managed to sustain just as the book was finally coming together.

I am forever grateful to my partner in craft and sister from another mister, Jessye. You know you have a true friend when she's prepared to spend the weekend with you sewing up a huge granny square blanket and weaving in the ends.

To my amazing children, who are beyond babies now, but will always be my little ones, Maya and Rishi. You inspired me to create, were my first models and have definitely inherited crafty little genes. Thank you for your patience when Mummy's mind was on a million other things, and also for not interrupting me when I was counting stitches.

To my husband, Kev, you've coped with me turning our home into some kind of woolly escape room and I know you have no idea how the whole crocheting thing works but you've always encouraged and supported me, especially on the days when I didn't think I could do it. I'm a lucky girl, thanks for persisting with me.